Contents

Introduction

This anthology has been prepared to support the following International General Certificate of Secondary Education (International GCSE) specifications:

- Edexcel International GCSE in English Language (Specification A) (4EA0)
- Edexcel Level 1/Level 2 Certification in English Language (KEA0)
- Edexcel International GCSE in English Literature (4TE0)
- Edexcel Level 1/Level 2 Certificate in English Literature (KET0).

International GCSE in English Language (Specification A)

Students studying the Edexcel International GCSE in English Language (Specification A) must study all the texts in Section A of this anthology in preparation for Paper 1 where they will be tested for Reading and Writing. Copies of this anthology must **not** be taken into the examination, the anthology text set for the paper will be reprinted on the examination paper.

Students following Route 1 (100 per cent assessment) must study **all** the texts in Section B of this anthology in preparation for Paper 2 where they will be tested for Reading. Copies of this anthology must not be taken into the examination, the anthology text set for the paper will be reprinted on the examination paper.

Students following Route 2 (Edexcel-approved teaching institutions only) will need to produce a coursework assignment responding to a piece, or pieces, from Section B of this anthology. To prepare for this they should study all the texts in Section B.

Further information is given in the specification which must be read in conjunction with this anthology.

Edexcel Level 1/Level 2 Certificate in English Language

Students must study **all** texts in Section A in preparation for paper 1. Copies of the anthology must **not** be taken into the examination, the anthology text set for the paper will be reprinted on the examination paper.

Students must study **all** the texts in Section B of this anthology in preparation for Paper 2 where they will be tested for Reading. Copies of this anthology must **not** be taken into the examination, the anthology text set for the paper will be reprinted on the examination paper.

International GCSE in English Literature

Students studying the Edexcel International GCSE in English Literature must study **all** the poems in Section C of this anthology in preparation for either Paper 2 or Component 3.

Students following Route 1 (100 per cent assessment) will be set three questions and they must answer one. Two of the questions set will be on poems studied in Section C. Copies of this anthology must **not** be taken into the examination, all the anthology poems will be reprinted for the examination paper in a separate booklet.

Students following Route 2 (Edexcel-approved teaching institutions only) will need to produce a coursework assignment responding to at least three poems in detail from Section C of this anthology. They must also refer to a further three poems which do not have to be from the anthology. To prepare for this they should study all the poems in Section C.

Further information is given in the specification which must be read in conjunction with this anthology.

Edexcel Level 1/Level 2 Certificate in English Literature

Students must study **all** poems in Section C for paper 2. Copies of the anthology must **not** be taken into the examination, the anthology text set for the paper will be reprinted on the examination paper.

Section A

From Touching the Void

Joe and Simon are mountain climbing in the Andes, when Joe has a terrible accident. Here are two accounts by Joe and Simon of what happened.

Joe's account

I hit the slope at the base of the cliff before I saw it coming. I was facing into the slope and both knees locked as I struck it. I felt a shattering blow in my knee, felt bones splitting, and screamed. The impact catapulted me over backwards and down the slope of the East Face. I slid, head-first, on my back. The rushing speed of it confused me. I thought of the drop below but felt nothing. Simon would be ripped off the mountain. He couldn't hold this. I screamed again as I jerked to a sudden violent stop.

Everything was still, silent. My thoughts raced madly. Then pain flooded down my thigh — a fierce burning fire coming down the inside of my thigh, seeming to ball in my groin, building and building until I cried out at it, and my breathing came in ragged gasps. My leg! ... My leg!

I hung, head down, on my back, left leg tangled in the rope above me and my right leg hanging slackly to one side. I lifted my head from the snow and stared, up across my chest, at a grotesque distortion in the right knee, twisting the leg into a strange zigzag. I didn't connect it with the pain which burnt my groin. That had nothing to do with my knee. I kicked my left leg free of the rope and swung round until I was hanging against the snow on my chest, feet down. The pain eased. I kicked my left foot into the slope and stood up.

A wave of nausea surged over me. I pressed my face into the snow, and the sharp cold seemed to calm me. Something terrible, something dark with dread occurred to me, and as I thought about it I felt the dark thought break into panic: 'I've broken my leg, that's it. I'm dead. Everyone said it ... if there's just two of you a broken ankle could turn into a death sentence ... if it's broken ... if ... It doesn't hurt so much, maybe I've just ripped something.'

I kicked my right leg against the slope, feeling sure it wasn't broken. My knee exploded. Bone grated, and the fireball rushed from groin to knee. I screamed. I looked down at the knee and could see it was broken, yet I tried not to believe what I was seeing. It wasn't just broken, it was ruptured, twisted, crushed, and I could see the kink in the joint and knew what had happened. The impact had driven my lower leg up through the knee joint. ...

I dug my axes into the snow, and pounded my good leg deeply into the soft slope until I felt sure it wouldn't slip. The effort brought back the nausea and I felt my head spin giddily to the point of fainting. I moved and a searing spasm of pain cleared away the faintness. I could see the summit of Seria Norte away to the west. I was not far below it. The sight drove home how desperately things had changed. We were above 19,000 feet, still on the ridge, and very much alone. I looked south at the small rise I had hoped to scale quickly and it seemed to grow with every second that I stared. I would never get over it. Simon would not be able to get me up it. He would leave me. He had no choice. I held my breath, thinking about it. Left here? Alone? ... For an age I felt overwhelmed at the notion of being left; I felt like screaming, and I felt like swearing, but stayed silent. If I said a word, I would panic. I could feel myself teetering on the edge of it.

Simon's account

Joe had disappeared behind a rise in the ridge and began moving faster than I could go. I was glad we had put the steep section behind us at last. ... I felt tired and was grateful to be able to follow Joe's tracks instead of breaking trail*.

I rested a while when I saw that Joe had stopped moving. Obviously he had found an obstacle and I thought I would wait until he started moving again. When the rope moved again I trudged forward after it, slowly.

Suddenly there was a sharp tug as the rope lashed out taut across the slope. I was pulled forward several feet as I pushed my axes into the snow and braced myself for another jerk. Nothing happened. I knew that Joe had fallen, but I couldn't see him, so I stayed put. I waited for about ten minutes until the tautened rope went slack on the snow and I felt sure that Joe had got his weight off me. I began to move along his footsteps cautiously, half expecting something else to happen. I kept tensed up and ready to dig my axes in at the first sign of trouble.

As I crested the rise, I could see down a slope to where the rope disappeared over the edge of a drop. I approached slowly, wondering what had happened. When I reached the top of the drop I saw Joe below me. He had one foot dug in and was leaning against the slope with his face buried in the snow. I asked him what had happened and he looked at me in surprise. I knew he was injured, but the significance didn't hit me at first.

He told me very calmly that he had broken his leg. He looked pathetic, and my immediate thought came without any emotion. ... You're dead ... no two ways about it! I think he knew it too. I could see it in his face. It was all totally rational. I knew where we were, I took in everything around me instantly, and knew he was dead. It never occurred to me that I might also die. I accepted without question that I could get off the mountain alone. I had no doubt about that.

... Below him I could see thousands of feet of open face falling into the eastern glacier bay. I watched him quite dispassionately. I couldn't help him, and it occurred to me that in all likelihood he would fall to his death. I wasn't disturbed by the thought. In a way I hoped he would fall. I knew I couldn't leave him while he was still fighting for it, but I had no idea how I might help him. I could get down. If I tried to get him down I might die with him. It didn't frighten me. It just seemed a waste. It would be pointless. I kept staring at him, expecting him to fall ...

Joe Simpson

breaking trail: being in front

 UG026701 - Anthology for Edexcel International GCSE and Certificate Qualifications in English Language and Literature - Issue 2 - March 2012 © Pearson Education Limited 2012

Your Guide to Beach Safety

Adapted from the RNLI leaflet — On the Beach.

The sections of the RNLI leaflet that need to be studied are reproduced here. To see the leaflet in full visit the Edexcel website (www.edexcel.com/internationalgcse2009).

TRUE STORY

Carolyne Yard will never forget her holiday in June 2007

'It was our last day and I was relaxing on the beach with my daughter and friend Mark. My sons, Angus and Will, were swimming in the sea. But Mark noticed that the boys had been swept towards some rocks, and they started shouting for help. They're big teenagers who don't usually call for their mum so I knew something was seriously wrong.

'They were caught in a strong rip current, and they couldn't swim back to shore. The water was like a whirlpool. They were so close, and yet in so much trouble.

'Mark and a surfer called Mike got in the water to help while I dialled 999 for the Coastguard on my mobile phone. They called the RNLI lifeguards from the neighbouring beach. It only took minutes for the rescue boat to arrive, but when you think your boys are going to drown, it seems to take a lifetime. I lost sight of them, which was terrifying.

'One of the lifeguards, Bernadette, jumped into the water. Mike had helped Angus to get to one side of the current, and Bernadette helped them both up onto a rock. Then she guided Mark and Will out of the current and between the rocks.

'Angus and Will were shaking with shock. I was crying, and just so relieved that we were all back together safely. It still makes me cry when I think about it.

'I'll certainly always go to a lifeguard-patrolled beach in future, and I know the boys will too. I will be eternally grateful to the lifeguards – if they hadn't been there that day, my boys would have drowned.'

WILL AND
HIS MUM
REUNITED

RIPS

Rips are strong currents that can quickly take swimmers from the shallows out beyond their depth.

Lifeguards will show you where you can avoid rips but if you do get caught in one:
* Stay calm - don't panic.
* If you can stand, wade don't swim.
* Keep hold of your board or inflatable to help you float.
* Raise your hand and shout for help.
* Never try to swim directly against the rip or you'll get exhausted.
* Swim parallel to the beach until free of the rip, then make for shore.
* If you see anyone else in trouble, alert the lifeguards or call **999** or **112** and ask for the Coastguard.

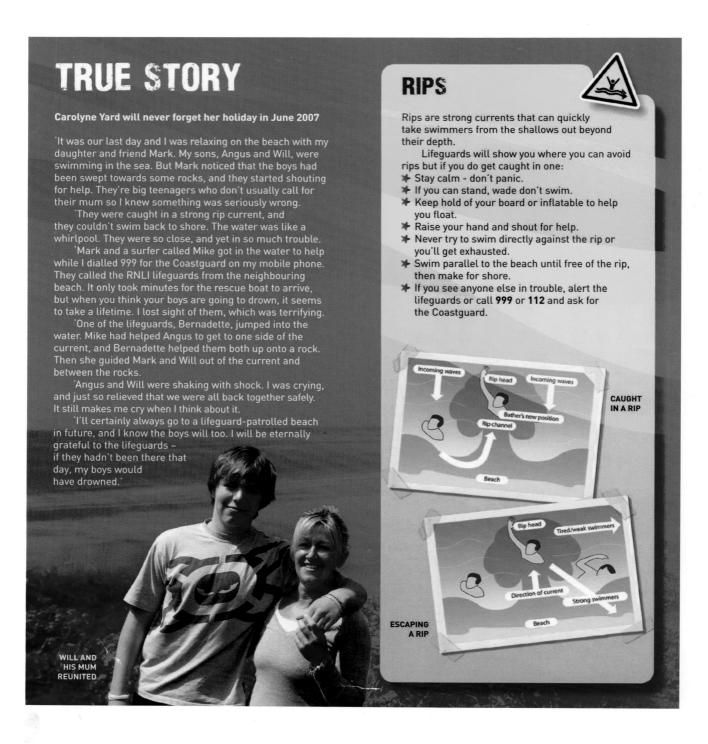

CAUGHT
IN A RIP

ESCAPING
A RIP

UG026701 – Anthology for Edexcel International GCSE and Certificate Qualifications in English Language and Literature – Issue 2 – March 2012 © Pearson Education Limited 2012

KNOW YOUR FLAGS

RED AND YELLOW FLAGS

These show the lifeguarded area, the safest place to swim, bodyboard and use inflatables.

BLACK AND WHITE CHEQUERED FLAGS

For surfboards, kayaks and other non-powered craft. Never swim or bodyboard here.

ORANGE WINDSOCK

Shows offshore winds so never use an inflatable when the sock is flying.

RED FLAG

Danger! **Never** go in the water when the red flag is up, under any circumstances.

If you see anyone else in trouble, alert the lifeguards or call **999** or **112** and ask for the Coastguard.

SWIMMING, SURFING & BODYBOARDING

Swimming is one of the best all-round activities you can do, but the sea is very different from being in a pool – even small waves can take you by surprise and disorientate you.

Surfing and bodyboarding are the most fantastic fun, but are very demanding, so you need to be a good swimmer. Experience of swimming at surf beaches is a great start, as it will help you develop an understanding of the behaviour of waves.

If you're new to the sport, we suggest you get some proper training from an approved British Surf Association school. Visit britsurf.co.uk for further information.

ALL BOARDERS

Always:
- follow the advice of the lifeguards
- check your board for damage before use
- wear your leash
- stay with your board and shout for help if in difficulty

Never:
- go alone
- ditch your board as it will keep you afloat.

SURFBOARDERS ONLY

Always:
- surf between the black and white flags (if present)

Never:
- surf between the red and yellow flags
- never drop in on another surfer

BODYBOARDERS ONLY

Always:
- bodyboard between the red and yellow flags
- wear short fins

If you get into difficulties, stick up your hand and shout for help – but never abandon your board.

THE RNLI

The Royal National Lifeboat Institution is the charity that saves lives at sea.

LIFEBOATS AND LIFEGUARDS

We operate over 230 lifeboat stations in the UK and RoI and have over 330 lifeboats in service, 24 hours a day, 365 days a year. Since the RNLI was founded in 1824, our volunteer lifeboat crews have saved more than 137,000 lives – rescuing around 8,000 people every year.

Our seasonal lifeguard service now operates on more than 100 beaches in the UK. It responds to more than 9,000 incidents a year and is planned to double its coverage by 2010.

FUNDED BY YOU

As a charity, the RNLI relies on voluntary financial support including legacies, which help fund 6 out of 10 launches. With more people using our beaches and seas, the demand on our services is greater than ever and our running costs average over £335,000 a day.

LIFESAVING ADVICE AND INFORMATION

A range of free resources and practical advice is available to promote sea, beach and commercial fishing safety and to support primary and secondary school teachers. For further information call **0800 543210** or visit **rnli.org.uk**.

ORDINARY PEOPLE, EXTRAORDINARY ACTS

People from all walks of life help the RNLI to save lives at sea. Thousands of volunteer crew members, shorehelpers, committee members and fundraisers give their time, skill and commitment. They are strongly supported by specialist staff.

Training is vital – it turns volunteers into lifesavers. Every year the RNLI delivers the highest quality of training at The Lifeboat College in Poole and at its lifeboat stations.

BEACHES NEED LIFEGUARDS

Our lifeguards work with lifeboat crews to provide a seamless rescue service from the beach to the open sea.

When someone is drowning in the surf seconds count, so we need expert lifesavers on the beach ready to act.

As much as 95% of our lifeguards' work is preventative – that is, they look out for potential problems before they develop into something worse, and give proactive advice and information to beachgoers.

The RNLI aims to continue expanding its lifeguard service across the whole country – but we can't achieve this without support from the public.

Every year it costs at least £450 to equip and £900 to train each lifeguard – will you help us meet that need?

Phone 0800 543210 or go to rnli.org.uk to donate now and help save lives at sea. Thank you.

Whether we're rescuing an offshore fisherman or a child swept out to sea, the RNLI exists to save **Life first**.

Climate Change webpage - Greenpeace UK

[Handwritten annotations on the image include:]
- logo
- happiness
- Bold type
- short sentence
- declarative stating a shocking fact
- nature
- statistics
- emotive adjective
- the inclusive pronoun
- inclusive
- repetition of catastrophic
- bold
- list of three
- use of coloured text
- Banner
- command
- capitals
- Punctuations
- rhetorical
- orange - sense of urgency
- effect of global warming
- related articles
- Clear structure
- understanding

[Webpage text, left navigation:]
Home
About Greenpeace
Latest news
What we do
▾ Climate change
   The problems
   The solutions
   What we are doing
   What you can do
   Videos
   Related links
▸ Forests
▸ Oceans
▸ Nuclear power
▸ Peace
▸ GM food
▸ Toxics
What you can do
Donate now
Media centre

Login | Register

Search

International

RSS | What is RSS?

Some rights reserved

[Top navigation:] Donate | Take action | Sign up for e-updates | email | GO›

[Main content:]

Home > What we do

Climate change

The world is warming up. Already 150,000 people are dying every year because of climate change and, within 50 years, one-third of all land-based species could face extinction. If we carry on the way we are now, by 2100 the planet will likely be hotter than it's been at any point in the past two million years.

But catastrophic climate change isn't inevitable. We know that climate change is caused by burning fossil fuels. The technologies that could dramatically reduce our dependence on fossil fuels – **decentralised energy**, **renewables** and **efficiency**, hybrid cars, efficient buildings – already exist and have been proven to work. If we start cutting our emissions now, using these ready-to-go technologies, then there is still a chance to avoid the most catastrophic impacts of climate change.

What we're lacking is real action. The government needs to put in place meaningful policies to urgently reduce emissions – and to act on them immediately. Under New Labour, carbon emissions have risen. The government is set to miss its own emissions targets. Whether through political cowardice or industry lobbying, the government is failing to put their words into action.

We're the last generation that can stop this global catastrophe, and we need your help.

What you can do

We can stop catastrophic climate change. We know what causes it, we have the technologies to prevent it, and there's a rapidly growing understanding of just how urgent the need for action is.

All that's missing is the action itself.

The government needs to put in place meaningful policies to urgently reduce emissions - and to act on them immediately. We need your help to persuade them. Together, we can stop climate chaos.

TAKE ACTION | **The problems** | **The solutions**

[Right sidebar:]

↻ TAKE ACTION

STOP HEATHROW EXPANSION
NO THIRD RUNWAY
ADD YOUR VOICE!

Serious about tackling climate change?
Join the roar of opposition to airport expansion

- The problem with aviation
- Aviation: frequently asked questions
- No 3rd runway - write to Gordon Brown
- The Heathrow Voices tour: dates & times
- Climate change: the convenient solution

Add your voice! »

📶 **Climate news**

- A nice bit of schadenfreude in the morning
- Ireland is banning the bulb, why can't we?
- Heating up in Bali
- US trying to destroy international efforts to save the climate
- Four thousand tonne oil spill in the North Sea

more »

[Footer:] contact us | privacy policy | print | rss feeds | help

Source: http://www.greenpeace.org.uk/climate

Climate Change: The Facts

Adapted from an article published in *The Guardian* newspaper supplement — Science Course Part III: The Earth (in association with the Science Museum)

The subject of global warming has become impossible to ignore. But what are its implications? And is mankind really to blame?

Twenty years ago global warming was a fringe subject — it seemed absurd that we could be having an effect on the Earth's climate. Today global warming has become a political hot potato and the majority of scientists agree that it is a reality and here to stay.

What is global warming?

Extra carbon dioxide [CO2] in the atmosphere enhances a natural process known as the greenhouse effect. Greenhouse gases, such as carbon dioxide, absorb heat and release it slowly. Without this process, Earth would be too cold for life to survive.

Over the past 200 years mankind has increased the proportion of greenhouse gases in the Earth's atmosphere, primarily by burning fossil fuels. The higher levels of greenhouse gases are causing our planet to warm — global warming.

Is global warming really caused by humans?

Since 1958 scientists at the Mauna Loa Observatory in Hawaii have taken continuous measurements of atmospheric carbon dioxide. The levels go up and down with the seasons, but overall they demonstrate a relentless rise.

Bubbles of gas from ice cores and the chemical composition of fossil shells provide us with a record of atmospheric carbon dioxide going back millions of years. There have been warm periods in the past where carbon dioxide was at levels similar to those seen today. However, the rate of change that we see today is exceptional: carbon dioxide levels have never risen so fast. By 2000 they were 17% higher than in 1959.

Accompanying this rapid increase in carbon dioxide we see a rise in average global temperatures. Warming in the past 100 years has caused about a 0.8C increase in global average temperature. Eleven of the 12 years in the period 1995-2006 rank among the top 12 warmest years since 1850.

There is little doubt that humanity is responsible for the rapid rise in carbon dioxide levels. The rise in temperatures that has accompanied our fossil fuel addiction seem too much of a coincidence to be just chance. Most people now agree that our actions are having an effect on Earth's climate.

How hot will it get?

Estimates from some of the world's best climate scientists — the Intergovernmental Panel on Climate Change (IPCC) — suggest that the average global temperature will have risen between 2.5C and 10.4C by 2100.

Whether it will be the lower or upper end of this estimate is unclear. Currently, oceans and trees are helping to mop up some of the heat by absorbing carbon dioxide, but eventually they will reach capacity and be unable to absorb more. At this point the atmosphere will take the full load, potentially pushing temperatures sky high.

Is it just carbon dioxide we need to worry about?

No. Carbon dioxide is just one of a number of greenhouse gases, which include water vapour, methane, nitrous oxide and ozone. Livestock farming (farting cows) and rice paddy farming (rotting vegetation) have contributed to higher levels of methane in the atmosphere.

What is more, methane has a nasty sting in its tail. Although it only hangs around in the atmosphere for about 10 years, it is far more potent as a greenhouse gas, trapping about 20 times as much heat as carbon dioxide.

What are tipping points?

A steady rise in greenhouse gases won't necessarily cause a steady rise in global temperatures. Earth's climate is highly complicated and scientists fear that many delicate thresholds exist, which once passed could trigger a dramatic change. These thresholds have become known as "tipping points".

One potential trigger could be the release of methane from methane clathrate compounds buried on the sea floor. Currently these deposits are frozen, but if the oceans warm sufficiently they could melt, burping vast quantities of methane into the atmosphere. Scientists fear that this sudden release may cause a runaway greenhouse effect.

How will global warming affect us?

Although average global temperatures are predicted to rise, this doesn't necessarily mean that we'll be sitting in our deckchairs all year round. The extra energy from the added warmth in the Earth's atmosphere will need to find a release, and the result is likely to be more extreme weather.

If we stop emitting CO2 now will it get better straight away?

Unfortunately not. Research shows that we are already committed to an average global temperature rise of nearly 1C, lasting for at least the next 500 years.

Kate Ravilious

What is global warming?

What determines the temperature of the earth?

Solar energy emitted from the sun radiates to the Earth

Invisible infrared energy is radiated from the Earth to outer space

The temperature of the Earth results from the balance of these two

The greenhouse effect on the atmosphere

SOURCE: HADLEY CENTRE

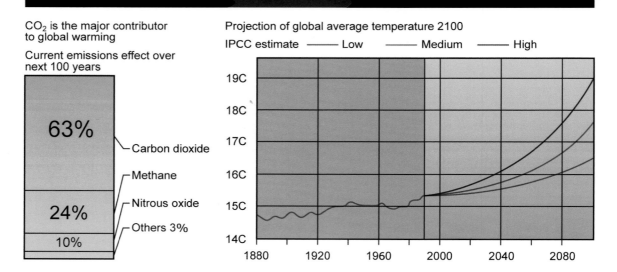

3 Most escapes to outer space and cools the Earth

1 Sunlight passes through the atmosphere and warms the Earth

2 Infrared radiation is given off by the Earth

4 Some IR is trapped by gasses in the air thus reducing the cooling

CO_2 is the major contributor to global warming

Current emissions effect over next 100 years

63% — Carbon dioxide

24% — Methane — Nitrous oxide

10% — Others 3%

Projection of global average temperature 2100

IPCC estimate —— Low —— Medium —— High

19C
18C
17C
16C
15C
14C

1880   1920   1960   2000   2040   2080

From A Game of Polo with a Headless Goat

Emma Levine travelled throughout Asia researching and filming unusual sports. In this passage she writes about a donkey race in Karachi.

sarcasm

We drove off to find the best viewing spot, which turned out to be the crest of the hill so we could see the approaching race. I asked the lads if we could join in the 'Wacky Races' and follow the donkeys, and they loved the idea. 'We'll open the car boot, you climb inside and point your camera towards the race. As the donkeys overtake us, we'll join the cars.' 'But will you try and get to the front?' 'Oh yes, that's no problem.'

The two lads who had never been interested in this Karachi sport were suddenly fired up with enthusiasm. We waited for eternity on the brow of the hill, me perched in the boot with a zoom lens pointing out. Nearly one hour later I was beginning to

10 feel rather silly when the only action was a villager on a wobbly bicycle, who nearly fell off as he cycled past and gazed around at us.

Several vehicles went past, and some donkey-carts carrying spectators. 'Are they coming?' we called out to them. 'Coming, coming,' came the reply. I was beginning to lose faith in its happening, but the lads remained confident. *repetition*

Just as I was assuming that the race had been cancelled, we spotted two approaching donkey-carts in front of a cloud of fumes and dust created by some fifty vehicles roaring up in their wake. As they drew nearer, Yaqoob revved up the engine and began to inch the car out of the lay-by. The two donkeys were almost dwarfed by their entourage; but there was no denying their speed — the Kibla donkey is said

20 to achieve speeds of up to 40 kph, and this looked close. The two were neck-and-neck, their jockeys perched on top of the tiny carts using their whips energetically, although not cruelly. *rule of three*

The noise of the approaching vehicles grew; horns tooting, bells ringing, and the special rattles used just for this purpose (like maracas, a metal container filled with dried beans). Men standing on top of their cars and vans, hanging out of taxis and perched on lorries, all cheered and shouted, while the vehicles jostled to get to the front of the convoy.

Yaqoob chose exactly the right moment to edge out of the road and swerve in front of the nearest car, finding the perfect place to see the two donkeys and at the

30 front of the vehicles. This was Formula One without rules, or a city-centre rush hour gone anarchic; a complete flouting of every type of traffic rule and common sense.

Our young driver relished this unusual test of driving skills. It was survival of the fittest, and depended upon the ability to cut in front of a vehicle with a sharp flick of the steering wheel (no lane discipline here); quick reflexes to spot a gap in the traffic for a couple of seconds; nerves of steel, and an effective horn. There were *rule of three* two races — the motorized spectators at the back; in front, the two donkeys, still running close and amazingly not put off by the uproar just behind them. Ahead of the donkeys, oncoming traffic — for it was a main road — had to dive into the ditch and wait there until we had passed. Yaqoob loved it. We stayed near to the front, his *dashes*

40 hand permanently on the horn and his language growing more colourful with every *Punctuation* vehicle that tried to cut in front. ...

The road straightened and levelled, and everyone picked up speed as we neared the end of the race. But just as they were reaching the finishing line, the hospital gate, there was a near pile-up as the leading donkey swerved, lost his footing and he and the cart tumbled over. The race was over.

And then the trouble began. I assumed the winner was the one who completed the race but it was not seen that way by everyone. Apart from the two jockeys and 'officials' (who, it turned out, were actually monitoring the race) there were over a hundred punters who had all staked money on the race, and therefore had strong
50 opinions. Some were claiming that the donkey had fallen because the other one had been ridden too close to him. Voices were raised, fists were out and tempers rising. Everyone gathered around one jockey and official, while the bookmakers were trying to insist that the race should be re-run.

Yaqoob and Iqbal were nervous of hanging around a volatile situation. They agreed to find out for me what was happening ordering me to stay inside the car as they were swallowed up by the crowd. They emerged sometime later. 'It's still not resolved,' said Iqbal, 'but it's starting to get nasty. I think we should leave.' As we drove away, Yaqoob reflected on his driving skills. 'I really enjoyed that,' he said as we drove off at a more sedate pace. 'But I don't even have my licence yet because
60 I'm underage!'

They both found this hilarious, but I was glad he hadn't told me before; an inexperienced, underage driver causing a massive pile-up in the middle of the high-stakes donkey race could have caused problems.

Emma Levine

From A Passage to Africa

George Alagiah writes about his experiences as a television reporter during the war in Somalia, Africa in the 1990s. He won a special award for his report on the incidents described in this passage.

I saw a thousand hungry, lean, scared and betrayed faces as I criss-crossed Somalia between the end of 1991 and December 1992, but there is one I will never forget.

I was in a little hamlet just outside Gufgaduud, a village in the back of beyond, a place the aid agencies had yet to reach. In my notebook I had jotted down instructions on how to get there. 'Take the Badale Road for a few kilometres till the end of the tarmac, turn right on to a dirt track, stay on it for about forty-five minutes — Gufgaduud. Go another fifteen minutes approx. — like a ghost village.' ...

In the ghoulish manner of journalists on the hunt for the most striking pictures, my cameraman ... and I tramped from one hut to another. What might have appalled
10 us when we'd started our trip just a few days before no longer impressed us much. The search for the shocking is like the craving for a drug: you require heavier and more frequent doses the longer you're at it. Pictures that stun the editors one day are written off as the same old stuff the next. This sounds callous, but it is just a fact of life. It's how we collect and compile the images that so move people in the comfort of their sitting rooms back home.

There was Amina Abdirahman, who had gone out that morning in search of wild, edible roots, leaving her two young girls lying on the dirt floor of their hut. They had been sick for days, and were reaching the final, enervating stages of terminal hunger. Habiba was ten years old and her sister, Ayaan, was nine. By the time Amina
20 returned, she had only one daughter. Habiba had died. No rage, no whimpering, just a passing away — that simple, frictionless, motionless deliverance from a state of half-life to death itself. It was, as I said at the time in my dispatch, a vision of 'famine away from the headlines, a famine of quiet suffering and lonely death'.

There was the old woman who lay in her hut, abandoned by relations who were too weak to carry her on their journey to find food. It was the smell that drew me to her doorway: the smell of decaying flesh. Where her shinbone should have been there was a festering wound the size of my hand. She'd been shot in the leg as the retreating army of the deposed dictator ... took revenge on whoever it found in its way. The shattered leg had fused into the gentle V-shape of a boomerang. It was
30 rotting; she was rotting. You could see it in her sick, yellow eyes and smell it in the putrid air she recycled with every struggling breath she took.

And then there was the face I will never forget.

My reaction to everyone else I met that day was a mixture of pity and revulsion*. Yes, revulsion. The degeneration of the human body, sucked of its natural vitality by the twin evils of hunger and disease, is a disgusting thing. We never say so in our TV reports. It's a taboo that has yet to be breached. To be in a feeding centre is to hear and smell the excretion of fluids by people who are beyond controlling their bodily functions. To be in a feeding centre is surreptitiously* to wipe your hands on the back of your trousers after you've held the clammy palm of a mother who has just cleaned
40 vomit from her child's mouth.

There's pity, too, because even in this state of utter despair they aspire to a dignity that is almost impossible to achieve. An old woman will cover her shrivelled body with a soiled cloth as your gaze turns towards her. Or the old and dying man who keeps his hoe next to the mat with which, one day soon, they will shroud his corpse, as if he means to go out and till the soil once all this is over.

I saw that face for only a few seconds, a fleeting meeting of eyes before the face turned away, as its owner retreated into the darkness of another hut. In those brief moments there had been a smile, not from me, but from the face. It was not a smile of greeting, it was not a smile of joy — how could it be? — but it was a smile
50 nonetheless. It touched me in a way I could not explain. It moved me in a way that went beyond pity or revulsion.

What was it about that smile? I had to find out. I urged my translator to ask the man why he had smiled. He came back with an answer. 'It's just that he was embarrassed to be found in this condition,' the translator explained. And then it clicked. That's what the smile had been about. It was the feeble smile that goes with apology, the kind of smile you might give if you felt you had done something wrong.

Normally inured* to stories of suffering, accustomed to the evidence of deprivation, I was unsettled by this one smile in a way I had never been before. There is an unwritten code between the journalist and his subjects in these
60 situations. The journalist observes, the subject is observed. The journalist is active, the subject is passive. But this smile had turned the tables on that tacit agreement. Without uttering a single word, the man had posed a question that cut to the heart of the relationship between me and him, between us and them, between the rich world and the poor world. If he was embarrassed to be found weakened by hunger and ground down by conflict, how should I feel to be standing there so strong and confident?

I resolved there and then that I would write the story of Gufgaduud with all the power and purpose I could muster. It seemed at the time, and still does, the only adequate answer a reporter can give to the man's question.

70 I have one regret about that brief encounter in Gufgaduud. Having searched through my notes and studied the dispatch that the BBC broadcast, I see that I never found out what the man's name was. Yet meeting him was a seminal moment in the gradual collection of experiences we call context. Facts and figures are the easy part of journalism. Knowing where they sit in the great scheme of things is much harder. So, my nameless friend, if you are still alive, I owe you one.

George Alagiah

*revulsion: disgust

*surreptitiously: secretly

*inured: hardened

From The Explorer's Daughter

As a small child, Kari Herbert lived, with her family, among the Inughuit people (sometimes called Eskimos) in the harsh environment of the Arctic. In 2002 she revisited the area, staying near Thule, a remote settlement in the snowy wastes of north Greenland. In this passage she writes about her experience of watching a hunt for the narwhal, a toothed whale, and what she thought and felt about it.

Two hours after the last of the hunters had returned and eaten, narwhal were spotted again, this time very close. Within an hour even those of us on shore could with the naked eye see the plumes of spray from the narwhal catching the light in a spectral play of colour. Two large pods* of narwhal circled in the fjord*, often looking as if they were going to merge, but always slowly, methodically passing each other by. Scrambling back up to the lookout I looked across the glittering kingdom in front of me and took a sharp intake of breath. The hunters were dotted all around the fjord. The evening light was turning butter-gold, glinting off man and whale and catching the soft billows of smoke from a lone hunter's pipe. From where we sat at
10 the lookout it looked as though the hunters were close enough to touch the narwhal with their bare hands and yet they never moved. Distances are always deceptive in the Arctic, and I fell to wondering if the narwhal existed at all or were instead mischievous tricks of the shifting light. ...

The narwhal rarely stray from High Arctic waters, escaping only to the slightly more temperate waters towards the Arctic Circle in the dead of winter, but never entering the warmer southern seas. In summer the hunters of Thule are fortunate to witness the annual return of the narwhal to the Inglefield Fjord, on the side of which we now sat.

The narwhal ... is an essential contributor to the survival of the hunters in the
20 High Arctic. The mattak or blubber* of the whale is rich in necessary minerals and vitamins, and in a place where the climate prohibits the growth of vegetables or fruit, this rich source of vitamin C was the one reason that the Eskimos have never suffered from scurvy*. ... For centuries the blubber of the whales was also the only source of light and heat, and the dark rich meat is still a valuable part of the diet for both man and dogs (a single narwhal can feed a team of dogs for an entire month). Its single ivory tusk, which can grow up to six feet in length, was used for harpoon tips and handles for other hunting implements (although the ivory was found to be brittle and not hugely satisfactory as a weapon), for carving protective tupilaks*, and even as a central beam for their small ancient dwellings. Strangely, the tusk seems
30 to have little use for the narwhal itself; they do not use the tusk to break through ice as a breathing hole, nor will they use it to catch or attack prey, but rather the primary use seems to be to disturb the top of the sea bed in order to catch Arctic halibut for which they have a particular predilection*. Often the ends of their tusks are worn down or even broken from such usage.

The women clustered on the knoll of the lookout, binoculars pointing in every direction, each woman focusing on her husband or family member, occasionally spinning round at a small gasp or jump as one of the women saw a hunter near a narwhal. ... Each wife knew her husband instinctively and watched their progress intently; it was crucial to her that her husband catch a narwhal — it was part of their
40 staple diet, and some of the mattak and meat could be sold to other hunters who hadn't been so lucky, bringing in some much-needed extra income. Every hunter was on the water. It was like watching a vast, waterborne game with the hunters spread like a net around the sound.

The narwhal … are intelligent creatures, their senses are keen and they talk to one another under the water. Their hearing is particularly developed and they can hear the sound of a paddling kayak from a great distance. That … was why the hunters had to sit so very still in the water.

One hunter was almost on top of a pair of narwhal, and they were huge. He gently picked up his harpoon and aimed — in that split second my heart leapt for
50   both hunter and narwhal. I urged the man on in my head; he was so close, and so brave to attempt what he was about to do — he was miles from land in a flimsy kayak, and could easily be capsized and drowned. The hunter had no rifle, only one harpoon with two heads and one bladder. It was a foolhardy exercise and one that could only inspire respect. And yet at the same time my heart also urged the narwhal to dive, to leave, to survive.

This dilemma stayed with me the whole time that I was in Greenland. I understand the harshness of life in the Arctic and the needs of the hunters and their families to hunt and live on animals and sea mammals that we demand to be protected because of their beauty. And I know that one cannot afford to be
60   sentimental in the Arctic. 'How can you possibly eat seal?' I have been asked over and over again. True, the images that bombarded us several years ago of men battering seals for their fur hasn't helped the issue of polar hunting, but the Inughuit do not kill seals using this method, nor do they kill for sport. They use every part of the animals they kill, and most of the food in Thule is still brought in by the hunter-gatherers and fishermen. Imported goods can only ever account for part of the food supply; there is still only one annual supply ship that makes it through the ice to Qaanaaq, and the small twice-weekly plane from West Greenland can only carry a certain amount of goods. Hunting is still an absolute necessity in Thule.

Kari Herbert

*pods**: small groups of whales

*fjord**: a long, narrow inlet of the sea with steep sides

*mattak or blubber**: the fatty skin of the whale

*scurvy**: a painful, weakening disease caused by lack of vitamin C

*tupilaks**: figures with magical powers, charms

*predilection**: liking

Explorers, or boys messing about? Either way, taxpayer gets rescue bill

Adapted from an article published in *The Guardian* newspaper, Tuesday January 28 2003

Helicopter duo plucked from liferaft after Antarctic crash

Their last expedition ended in farce when the Russians threatened to send in military planes to intercept them as they tried to cross into Siberia via the icebound Bering Strait.

Yesterday a new adventure undertaken by British explorers Steve Brooks and Quentin Smith almost led to tragedy when their helicopter plunged into the sea off Antarctica.

The men were plucked from the icy water by a Chilean naval ship after a nine-hour rescue which began when Mr Brooks contacted his wife, Jo Vestey, on his satellite phone asking for assistance. The rescue involved the Royal Navy, the RAF and British coastguards.

Last night there was resentment in some quarters that the men's adventure had cost the taxpayers of Britain and Chile tens of thousands of pounds.

Experts questioned the wisdom of taking a small helicopter — the four-seater Robinson R44 has a single engine — into such a hostile environment.

There was also confusion about what exactly the men were trying to achieve. A website set up to promote the Bering Strait expedition claims the team were planning to fly from the north to south pole in their "trusty helicopter".

But Ms Vestey claimed she did not know what the pair were up to, describing them as "boys messing about with a helicopter".

The drama began at around 1am British time when Mr Brooks, 42, and 40-year-old Mr Smith, also known as Q, ditched into the sea 100 miles off Antarctica, about 36 miles north of Smith Island, and scrambled into their liferaft.

Mr Brooks called his wife in London on his satellite phone. She said: "He said they were both in the liferaft but were okay and could I call the emergency people?"

Meanwhile, distress signals were being beamed from the ditched helicopter and from Mr Brooks' Breitling emergency watch, a wedding present.

The signals from the aircraft were deciphered by Falmouth* coastguard and passed on to the rescue coordination centre at RAF Kinloss in Scotland.

The Royal Navy's ice patrol ship, HMS Endurance, which was 180 miles away surveying uncharted waters, began steaming towards the scene and dispatched its two Lynx helicopters.

One was driven back because of poor visibility but the second was on its way when the men were picked up by a Chilean naval vessel at about 10.20am British time.

Though the pair wore survival suits and the weather at the spot where they ditched was clear, one Antarctic explorer told Mr Brooks' wife it was "nothing short of a miracle" that they had survived.

Both men are experienced adventurers. Mr Brooks, a property developer from London, has taken part in expeditions to 70 countries in 15 years. He has trekked solo to Everest base camp and walked barefoot for three days in the Himalayas. He has negotiated the white water rapids of the Zambezi river by kayak and survived a charge by a silver back gorilla in the Congo. He is also a qualified mechanical engineer and pilot.

He and his wife spent their honeymoon flying the helicopter from Alaska to Chile. The 16,000-mile trip took three months.

Mr Smith, also from London, claims to have been flying since the age of five. He has twice flown a helicopter around the globe and won the world freestyle helicopter flying championship.

Despite their experience, it is not the first time they have hit the headlines for the wrong reasons.

In April, Mr Brooks and another explorer, Graham Stratford, were poised to become the first to complete a crossing of the 56-mile wide frozen Bering Strait between the US and Russia in an amphibious vehicle, Snowbird VI, which could carve its way through ice floes and float in the water in between.

But they were forced to call a halt after the Russian authorities told them they would scramble military helicopters to lift them off the ice if they crossed the border.

Ironically, one of the aims of the expedition, for which Mr Smith provided air back-up, was to demonstrate how good relations between east and west had become.

The wisdom of the team's latest adventure was questioned by, among others, Günter Endres, editor of Jane's Helicopter Markets and Systems, said: "I'm surprised they used the R44. I wouldn't use a helicopter like that to go so far over the sea. It sounds as if they were pushing it to the maximum".

A spokesman for the pair said it was not known what had gone wrong. The flying conditions had been "excellent".

The Ministry of Defence said the taxpayer would pick up the bill, as was normal in rescues in the UK and abroad. The spokesperson said it was "highly unlikely" it would recover any of the money.

Last night the men were on their way to the Chilean naval base Eduardo Frei, where HMS Endurance was to pick them up. Ms Vestey said: "They have been checked and appear to be well. I don't know what will happen to them once they have been picked up by HMS Endurance — they'll probably have their bottoms kicked and be sent home the long way".

Steven Morris

*Falmouth**: coastal town in Cornwall, England

UG026701 - Anthology for Edexcel International GCSE and Certificate Qualifications in English Language and Literature - Issue 2 - March 2012 © Pearson Education Limited 2012

From Taking on the World

Ellen MacArthur became famous in 2001 when she competed in the Vendée Globe solo round-the-world yacht race. She was the youngest (24 years old) and probably the shortest (just 5ft 2in!) competitor. She came second, despite appalling weather, exhaustion and, as she describes here, problems with her boat.

I climbed the mast on Christmas Eve, and though I had time to get ready, it was the hardest climb to date. I had worked through the night preparing for it, making sure I had all the tools, mouse lines* and bits I might need, and had agonized for hours over how I should prepare the halyard* so that it would stream out easily below me and not get caught as I climbed.

When it got light I decided that the time was right. I kitted up in my middle-layer clothes as I didn't want to wear so much that I wouldn't be able to move freely up there. The most dangerous thing apart from falling off is to be thrown against the mast, and though I would be wearing a helmet it would not be difficult to break
10 bones up there. ...

I laid out the new halyard on deck, flaking it neatly so there were no twists. As I took the mast in my hands and began to climb I felt almost as if I was stepping on to the moon — a world over which I had no control. You can't ease the sheets* or take a reef*, nor can you alter the settings for the autopilot. If something goes wrong you are not there to attend to it. You are a passive observer looking down at your boat some 90 feet below you. After climbing just a couple of metres I realized how hard it was going to be, I couldn't feel my fingers — I'd need gloves, despite the loss in dexterity. I climbed down, getting soaked as we ploughed into a wave — the decks around my feet were awash. I unclipped my jumar* from the halyard and put on a
20 pair of sailing gloves. There would be no second climb on this one — I knew that I would not have the energy.

As I climbed my hands were more comfortable, and initially progress was positive. But it got harder and harder as I was not only pulling my own weight up as I climbed but also the increasingly heavy halyard — nearly 200 feet of rope by the time I made it to the top. The physical drain came far less from the climbing than from the clinging on. The hardest thing is just to hang on as the mast slices erratically through the air. There would be the odd massive wave which I could feel us surf down, knowing we would pile into the wave in front. I would wrap my arms around the mast and press my face against its cold and slippery carbon surface, waiting for the
30 shuddering slowdown. Eyes closed and teeth gritted, I hung on tight, wrists clenched together, and hoped. Occasionally on the smaller waves I would be thrown before I could hold on tight, and my body and the tools I carried were thrown away from the mast; I'd be hanging on by just one arm, trying to stop myself from smacking back into the rig.

By the third spreader* I was exhausted; the halyard was heavier and the motion more violent. I held on to her spreader base and hung there, holding tight to breathe more deeply and conjure up more energy. But I realized that the halyard was tight and that it had caught on something. ... I knew that if I went down to free it I would not have the energy to climb up once again. I tugged and tugged on the rope — the
40   frustration was unreal. It had to come, quite simply the rope had to come free. Luckily with all the pulling I managed to create enough slack to make it to the top, but now I was even more exhausted. I squinted at the grey sky above me and watched the mast-head whip across the clouds. The wind whistled past us, made visible by the snow that had begun to fall. Below the sea stretched out for ever, the size and length of the waves emphasized by this new aerial view. This is what it must look like to the albatross.

I rallied once more and left the safety of the final spreader for my last hike to the top. The motion was worse than ever, and as I climbed I thought to myself, not far now, kiddo, come on, just keep moving ... As the mast-head came within reach
50   there was a short moment of relief; at least there was no giving up now I had made it — whatever happened now I had the whole mast to climb down. I fumbled at the top of the rig, feeding in the halyard and connecting the other end to the top of *Kingfisher*'s mast. The job only took half an hour — then I began my descent. This was by far the most dangerous part and I had my heart in my mouth — no time for complacency now, I thought, not till you reach the deck, kiddo, it's far from over...

It was almost four hours before I called Mark back and I shook with exhaustion as we spoke. We had been surfing at well over 20 knots while I was up there. My limbs were bruised and my head was spinning, but I felt like a million dollars as I spoke on the phone. Santa had called on *Kingfisher* early and we had the best present ever —
60   a new halyard.

Ellen MacArthur

*mouse line**: length of wire wrapped across the mouth of a hook, or through a shackle pin and around the shackle, for the sake of security

*halyard**: a rope used for raising and lowering sails

*sheet**: a line to control the sails

*reef**: reduces area of sails

*jumar**: a climbing device that grips the rope so that it can be climbed

*spreader**: a bar attached to a yacht's mast

From Chinese Cinderella

Growing up in a wealthy family in 1950s Hong Kong, Adeline Yen Mah should have had an enviable childhood, but she was rejected by her dominating stepmother and despised by her brothers and sisters. She was sent to a boarding school and left there. In this extract from her autobiography she relates one of the few occasions when she went home.

[handwritten annotations: depress and wistful tone / time is going too fast for her Preference]

Time went by relentlessly and it was Saturday again. Eight weeks more and it would be the end of term ... in my case perhaps the end of school forever. *[handwritten: foreboding creates tension]*

[handwritten: Pathetic fallacy / The weather is affecting her current state] Four of us were playing Monopoly. My heart was not in it and I was losing steadily. Outside it was hot and there was a warm wind blowing. The radio warned of a possible typhoon the next day. It was my turn and I threw the dice. As I played, the thought of leaving school throbbed at the back of my mind like a persistent toothache. *[handwritten: Metaphor – Pain is almost Physical]*

'Adeline!' Ma-mien Valentino was calling.

10 'You can't go now,' Mary protested. 'For once I'm winning. One, two, three, four. Good! You've landed on my property. Thirty-five dollars, please. Oh, good afternoon, Mother Valentino!'

We all stood up and greeted her.

'Adeline, didn't you hear me call you? Hurry up downstairs! Your chauffeur is waiting to take you home!'

Full of foreboding, I ran downstairs as in a nightmare, wondering who had died this time. Father's chauffeur assured me everyone was healthy. *[handwritten: Chauffeur is more aware about family situation than she is.]*

'Then why are you taking me home?' I asked.

'How should *I* know?' he answered defensively, shrugging his shoulders. 'Your guess is as good as mine. They give the orders and I carry them out.'

[handwritten: dread / instead of excitement]

20 During the short drive home, my heart was full of dread and I wondered what I had done wrong. Our car stopped at an elegant villa at mid-level, halfway up the hill between the peak and the harbour.

'Where are we?' I asked foolishly. *[handwritten: distant relationship]*

'Don't you know anything?' the chauffeur replied rudely. 'This is your new home. Your parents moved here a few months ago.'

[handwritten: cool not warm and quiet, isolation and distance.]

'I had forgotten,' I said as I got out.

Ah Gum opened the door. Inside, it was quiet and cool.

'Where is everyone?' *[handwritten: no family bonding]*

30 'Your mother is out playing bridge. Your two brothers and Little Sister are sunbathing by the swimming-pool. Your father is in his room and wants to see you as soon as you get home.'

'See me in his room?' I was overwhelmed by the thought that I had been summoned by Father to enter the Holy of Holies — a place to which I had never been invited. Why? ... *[handwritten: sacred place / short sentence, question mark and caesura to show build up of tension.]*

afraid

typical family roles

Timidly, I knocked on the door. Father was alone, looking relaxed in his slippers and bathrobe, reading a newspaper. He smiled as I entered and I saw he was in a happy mood. I breathed a small sigh of relief at first but became uneasy when I wondered why he was being so nice, thinking, Is this a giant ruse on his part to trick me? Dare I let my guard down?

40   'Sit down! Sit down!' He pointed to a chair. 'Don't look so scared. Here, take a look at this! They're writing about someone we both know, I think.'

He handed me the day's newspaper and there, in one corner, I saw my name ADELINE YEN in capital letters prominently displayed.

'It was announced today that 14-year-old Hong Kong schoolgirl ADELINE JUN-LING YEN of Sacred Heart Canossian School, Caine Road, Hong Kong, has won first prize in the International Play-writing Competition held in London, England, for the 1951—1952 school year. It is the first time that any local Chinese student from Hong Kong has won such a prestigious event. Besides a medal, the prize comes with a cash reward of FIFTY ENGLISH POUNDS. Our sincere congratulations, ADELINE YEN, for
50   bringing honour to Hong Kong. We are proud of you'.

Is it possible? Am I dreaming? Me, the winner?

'I was going up the lift this morning with my friend C.Y. Tung when he showed me this article and asked me, "Is the winner Adeline Jun-ling Yen related to you? The two of you have the same uncommon last name." Now C.Y. himself has a few children about your age but so far none of them has won an international literary prize, as far as I know. So I was quite pleased to tell him you are my daughter. Well done!'

He looked radiant. For once, he was proud of me. In front of his revered colleague, C.Y. Tung, a prominent fellow businessman also from Shanghai, I had
60   given him face. I thought, Is this the big moment I have been waiting for? My whole being vibrated with all the joy in the world. I only had to stretch out my hand to reach the stars.

'Tell me, how did you do it?' he continued. 'How come *you* won?'

'Well, the rules and regulations were so very complicated. One really has to be dedicated just to understand what they want. Perhaps I was the only one determined enough to enter and there were no other competitors!'

He laughed approvingly. 'I doubt it very much but that's a good answer.'

'Please, Father,' I asked boldly, thinking it was now or never. 'May I go to university in England too, just like my brothers?'

70   'I do believe you have potential. Tell me, what would you study?'

My heart gave a giant lurch as it dawned on me that he was agreeing to let me go. How marvellous it was simply to be alive! Study? I thought. Going to England is like entering heaven. Does it matter what you do after you get to heaven?

But Father was expecting an answer. What about creative writing? After all, I had just won first prize in an international writing competition!

'I plan to study literature. I'll be a writer.'

'Writer!' he scoffed. 'You are going to starve! What language are you going to write in and who is going to read your writing? Though you may think you're an expert in both Chinese and English, your Chinese is actually rather elementary. As for
80   your English, don't you think the native English speakers can write better than you?'

I waited in silence. I did not wish to contradict him.

'You will go to England with Third Brother this summer and you will go to medical school. After you graduate, you will specialise in obstetrics. Women will always be having babies. Women patients prefer women doctors. You will learn to deliver their babies. That's a foolproof profession for you. Don't you agree?'

Agree? Of course I agreed. Apparently, he had it all planned out. As long as he let me go to university in England, I would study anything he wished. How did that line go in Wordsworth's poem? *Bliss was it in that dawn to be alive*.

90 'Father, I shall go to medical school in England and become a doctor. Thank you very, very much.'

Adeline Yen Mah

Section B

UG026701 – Anthology for Edexcel International GCSE and Certificate Qualifications in English Language and Literature – Issue 2 – March 2012 © Pearson Education Limited 2012

Disabled

He sat in a wheeled chair, waiting for dark,
And shivered in his ghastly suit of grey,
Legless, sewn short at elbow. Through the park
Voices of boys rang saddening like a hymn,
5   Voices of play and pleasures after day,
Till gathering sleep had mothered them from him.

*   *   *

About this time Town used to swing so gay
When glow-lamps budded in the light-blue trees,
And girls glanced lovelier as the air grew dim —
10   In the old times, before he threw away his knees.
Now he will never feel again how slim
Girls' waists are, or how warm their subtle hands;
All of them touch him like some queer disease.

*   *   *

There was an artist silly for his face,
15   For it was younger than his youth, last year.
Now, he is old; his back will never brace;
He's lost his colour very far from here,
Poured it down shell-holes till the veins ran dry,
And half his lifetime lapsed in the hot race,
20   And leap of purple spurted from his thigh.

*   *   *

One time he liked a blood-smear down his leg,
After the matches, carried shoulder-high.
It was after football, when he'd drunk a peg,
He thought he'd better join. — He wonders why.
25   Someone had said he'd look a god in kilts,
That's why; and maybe, too, to please his Meg;
Aye, that was it, to please the giddy jilts
He asked to join. He didn't have to beg;

*   *   *

Smiling they wrote his lie; aged nineteen years.
30   Germans he scarcely thought of; all their guilt,
And Austria's, did not move him. And no fears
Of Fear came yet. He thought of jewelled hilts
For daggers in plaid socks; of smart salutes;
And care of arms; and leave; and pay arrears;
35   *Esprit de corps**; and hints for young recruits.
And soon he was drafted out with drums and cheers.

*   *   *

Some cheered him home, but not as crowds cheer Goal.
Only a solemn man who brought him fruits
Thanked him; and then inquired about his soul.

                    *   *   *

40   Now, he will spend a few sick years in Institutes,
        And do what things the rules consider wise,
        And take whatever pity they may dole.
        Tonight he noticed how the women's eyes
        Passed from him to the strong men that were whole.
45   How cold and late it is! Why don't they come
        And put him into bed? Why don't they come?

                                        Wilfred Owen

*Esprit de corps**: A feeling of pride in the group to which one belongs (French)

"Out, Out —"

The buzz saw snarled and rattled in the yard
And made dust and dropped stove-length sticks of wood,
Sweet-scented stuff when the breeze drew across it.
And from there those that lifted eyes could count
5   Five mountain ranges one behind the other
Under the sunset far into Vermont.
And the saw snarled and rattled, snarled and rattled,
As it ran light, or had to bear a load.
And nothing happened: day was all but done.
10   Call it a day, I wish they might have said
To please the boy by giving him the half hour
That a boy counts so much when saved from work.
His sister stood beside them in her apron
To tell them "Supper." At the word, the saw,
15   As if to prove saws knew what supper meant,
Leaped out at the boy's hand, or seemed to leap—
He must have given the hand. However it was,
Neither refused the meeting. But the hand!
The boy's first outcry was a rueful laugh,
20   As he swung toward them holding up the hand,
Half in appeal, but half as if to keep
The life from spilling. Then the boy saw all—
Since he was old enough to know, big boy
Doing a man's work, though a child at heart—
25   He saw all spoiled. "Don't let him cut my hand off—
The doctor, when he comes. Don't let him, sister!"
So. But the hand was gone already.
The doctor put him in the dark of ether.
He lay and puffed his lips out with his breath.
30   And then—the watcher at his pulse took fright.
No one believed. They listened at his heart.
Little—less—nothing!—and that ended it.
No more to build on there. And they, since they
Were not the one dead, turned to their affairs.

Robert Frost

[handwritten top: Blues rhyme and rhythm]

Refugee Blues *[handwritten: – written in 1939]*

[handwritten: spiritual/religious]
Say this city has ten million souls, *[handwritten: hyperbole]* *[handwritten: different people and their living conditions]*
Some are living in mansions, some are living in holes:
Yet there's no place for us, my dear, yet there's no place for us.

[handwritten: repetition – emphasises the difficulty faced by the couple.]

Once we had a country and we thought it fair,
5   Look in the atlas and you'll find it there: *[handwritten: A→A→B]*
We cannot go there now, my dear, we cannot go there now.

In the village churchyard there grows an old yew, *[handwritten: always new hope for nature, unlike refugees, natural metaphor.]*
Every spring it blossoms anew:
Old passports can't do that, my dear, old passports can't do that.

[handwritten: angry]
10   The consul banged the table and said:
"If you've got no passport you're officially dead": *[handwritten: metaphorically]*
But we are still alive, my dear, but we are still alive.

Went to a committee; they offered me a chair;
Asked me politely to return next year:
15   But where shall we go to-day, my dear, where shall we go to-day?

Came to a public meeting; the speaker got up and said: *[handwritten: using Christianity against the Jews.]*
"If we let them in, they will steal our daily bread";
He was talking of you and me, my dear, he was talking of you and me.

[handwritten: Pathetic fallacy (scary, threatening image)]
Thought I heard the thunder rumbling in the sky;
20   It was Hitler over Europe, saying: "They must die";
We were in his mind, my dear, we were in his mind.

Saw a poodle in a jacket fastened with a pin, *[handwritten: animals treated better]*
Saw a door opened and a cat let in:
But they weren't German Jews, my dear, but they weren't German Jews.

[handwritten: threat of death]
25   Went down to the harbour and stood upon the quay,
Saw the fish swimming as if they were free:
Only ten feet away, my dear, only ten feet away. *[handwritten: natural imagery]*

Walked through a wood, saw the birds in the trees;
They had no politicians and sang at their ease: *[handwritten: blame politicians]*
30   They weren't the human race, my dear, they weren't the human race.

Dreamed I saw a building with a thousand floors, *[handwritten: hopelessness]*
A thousand windows and a thousand doors;
Not one of them was ours, my dear, not one of them was ours.

[handwritten: pathetic fallacy / hyperbole]
Stood on a great plain in the falling snow;
35   Ten thousand soldiers marched to and fro: *[handwritten: German Jews]*
Looking for you and me, my dear, looking for you and me.

W. H. Auden

An Unknown Girl

In the evening bazaar
studded with neon
an unknown girl
is hennaing* my hand.
5   She squeezes a wet brown line
from a nozzle.
She is icing my hand,
which she steadies with hers
on her satin-peach knee.
10 In the evening bazaar
for a few rupees
an unknown girl
is hennaing my hand.
As a little air catches
15 my shadow-stitched kameez*
a peacock spreads its lines
across my palm.
Colours leave the street
float up in balloons.
20 Dummies in shop-fronts
tilt and stare
with their Western perms.
Banners for Miss India 1993,
for curtain cloth
25 and sofa cloth
canopy me.
I have new brown veins.
In the evening bazaar
very deftly
30 an unknown girl
is hennaing my hand.
I am clinging
to these firm peacock lines
like people who cling
35 to the sides of a train.
Now the furious streets
are hushed.
I'll scrape off
the dry brown lines
40 before I sleep,
reveal soft as a snail trail
the amber bird beneath.
It will fade in a week.
When India appears and reappears
45 I'll lean across a country
with my hands outstretched
longing for the unknown girl
in the neon bazaar.

Moniza Alvi

hennaing*: art of body decoration using a plant die
kameez*: loose fitting tunic

Electricity Comes to Cocoa Bottom

Then all the children of Cocoa Bottom
went to see Mr. Samuel's electric lights.
They camped on the grass bank outside his house,
their lamps filled with oil,
5   waiting for sunset,
watching the sky turn yellow, orange.
Grannie Patterson across the road
peeped through the crack in her porch door.
The cable was drawn like a pencil line across the sun.
10 The fireflies waited in the shadows,
their lanterns off.
The kling-klings* swooped in from the hills,
congregating in the orange trees.
A breeze coming home from sea held its breath;
15 bamboo lining the dirt road stopped its swaying,
and evening came as soft as chiffon curtains:
Closing. Closing.

Light!
Mr. Samuel smiling on the verandah —
20 a silhouette against the yellow shimmer behind him —
and there arising such a gasp,
such a fluttering of wings,
tweet-a-whit,
such a swaying, swaying.
25 Light! Marvellous light!
And then the breeze rose up from above the trees,
swelling and swelling into a wind
such that the long grass bent forward
stretching across the bank like so many bowed heads.
30 And a voice in the wind whispered:
Is there one among us to record this moment?
But there was none —

no one (except for a few warm rocks
35 hidden among mongoose ferns) even heard a sound.
Already the children of Cocoa Bottom
had lit their lamps for the dark journey home,
and it was too late —
the moment had passed.

Marcia Douglas

Kling-klings: birds

UG026701 - Anthology for Edexcel International GCSE and Certificate Qualifications in English Language
and Literature - Issue 2 - March 2012 © Pearson Education Limited 2012

The Last Night (from Charlotte Gray)

André and his brother Jacob are two orphaned boys in France in the 1940s. They are waiting to be taken to a concentration camp.

André was lying on the floor when a Jewish orderly came with postcards on which the deportees might write a final message. He advised them to leave them at the station or throw them from the train as camp orders forbade access to the post. Two or three pencils that had survived the barracks search were passed round among the people in the room. Some wrote with sobbing passion, some with punctilious care, as though their safety, or at least the way in which they were remembered, depended upon their choice of words.

A woman came with a sandwich for each child to take on the journey. She also had a pail of water, round which they clustered, holding out sardine cans they passed
10 from one to another. One of the older boys embraced her in his gratitude, but the bucket was soon empty.

When she was gone, there were only the small hours of the night to go through. André was lying on the straw, the soft bloom of his cheek laid, uncaring, in the dung. Jacob's limbs were intertwined with his for warmth.

The adults in the room sat slumped against the walls, wakeful and talking in lowered voices. Somehow, the children were spared the last hours of the wait by their ability to fall asleep where they lay, to dream of other places.

It was still the low part of the night when Hartmann and the head of another staircase came into the room with coffee. Many of the adults refused to drink
20 because they knew it meant breakfast, and therefore the departure. The children were at the deepest moments of their sleep.

Those who drank from the half dozen cups that circulated drank in silence. Then there went through the room a sudden ripple, a quickening of muscle and nerve as a sound came to them from below: it was the noise of an engine — a familiar sound to many of them, the homely thudding of a Parisian bus. ...

Five white-and-green municipal buses had come in through the main entrance, and now stood trembling in the wired-off corner of the yard. At a long table ... , the commandant of the camp himself sat with a list of names that another policeman was calling out in alphabetical order. In the place where its suburban destination was
30 normally signalled, each bus carried the number of a wagon on the eastbound train.

Many of the children were too deeply asleep to be roused, and those who were awake refused to come down when the gendarmes were sent up to fetch them. In the filthy straw they dug in their heels and screamed. ...

André heard his name and moved with Jacob towards the bus. From the other side of the courtyard, from windows open on the dawn, a shower of food was thrown towards them by women wailing and calling out their names, though none of the scraps reached as far as the enclosure.

André looked up, and in a chance angle of light he saw a woman's face in which the eyes were fixed with terrible ferocity on a child beside him. Why did she stare as
40 though she hated him? Then it came to André that she was not looking in hatred, but had kept her eyes so intensely open in order to fix the picture of her child in her mind. She was looking to remember, for ever.

He held on hard to Jacob as they mounted the platform of the bus. Some of the children were too small to manage the step up and had to be helped on by gendarmes, or pulled in by grown-ups already on board.

André's bus was given the signal to depart, but was delayed. A baby of a few weeks was being lifted on to the back, and the gendarme needed time to work the wooden crib over the passenger rail and into the crammed interior.

50   Eventually, the bus roared as the driver engaged the gear and bumped slowly out through the entrance, the headlights for a moment lighting up the café opposite before the driver turned the wheel and headed for the station.

Sebastian Faulks

Veronica

We had grown up together in my native village. Her family had been even poorer than mine, which was saying something in those days. Her father was a brute and her mother was weak, and since she was the eldest child a lot of the responsibility for bringing up the other children had fallen on her. From time to time I helped her out, but there was little I could do. Her father was a morbidly suspicious man. Visitors, apart from his drinking companions, were not encouraged, and I had no desire to be the cause of even more misery. I helped her fetch water from the stream and occasionally chopped firewood, but that was all. Night after night I would lie awake listening to her screams, cursing myself for my own physical inadequacy and my

10 father for his unwillingness to become involved.

When I was twelve I started at the secondary school in the town a few miles away. During term-time I stayed with my uncle, returning to the village only during the vacations. Veronica and I remained friendly, and she was always pleased to see me, and when we could we snatched time together by the stream and she asked me endless questions about my school and the town and what I was going to be when I grew up. But for all the misery of her own life she never seemed to envy me mine.

And then came the day when I was to leave for good. I had won a scholarship to the University and I knew in my heart I would be away a long time. I was eighteen then and I thought I knew my own worth. The day before I left we met by the

20 stream.

As she walked towards me I realized for the first time that she was no longer a girl anymore but a young woman. Her clothes were still shabby and if she was no great beauty she still had a certain attractiveness that I knew would appeal to some men. Not that she was likely to meet any as long as she remained where she was. And although her father had long since stopped beating her in every other respect nothing had really altered.

'You must be happy to be going,' she said. I shrugged and pretended to be unconcerned, but of course it was the break I had hardly dared hope for.

'What about you?' I asked.

30 'Me!'

'Yes, why don't you get out of this place? It has nothing to offer you.'

'I can't just leave my family.'

'Why not? What have they ever done for you?'

'Don't talk like that. They are my family, that is enough.'

'But think of all the things you can do in the city,' I said.

'No, the city is for you, not me. What will I do once I get there? I have no qualifications, not even Standard Six.'

Although I knew there was a lot of truth in what she said I resisted her arguments: I suppose I was both appalled and frightened by her fatalism.

40 'You can go to night school and become a secretary,' I said.

She shook her head. 'I leave that to others, my own place is here.'

I snapped a twig and threw it into the water. It bobbed on the current and then vanished from sight.

'When I have qualified I will send you money to take a correspondence course,' I said. She laughed.

'Don't talk <u>foolishness</u>,' she said and stood up. '<u>I have to go and cook, my father will be home soon.</u>' *The act of cooking is metaphor - her being the carer*

'Here is my address. If you need anything don't hesitate to write me.' I handed her a piece of paper. She took it and tucked it in her bosom. We said goodbye and
50 she hurried away. I thought I saw tears in her eyes as she turned to go, but I may have been mistaken. *shows me opportunities that education can provide*

<u>Well, I went to the city and made good.</u> I passed my exams and in due course I was ready to set up in a practice of my own. In all that time I did not return to the village: while I had been a student I lacked the time, and afterwards I lacked the inclination. As soon as it was possible for me to do so I sent for my parents to come and live with me and they settled down quickly enough to their new life.

But I never forgot Veronica. She was the only person I had asked about from my mother but she had merely shrugged her shoulders and said that nothing had changed. That was the trouble with village life: nothing ever changed.

60 It was ten years before I made the return journey. It was in connection with my work. The government had set up a scheme whereby all the doctors in the country were obliged to put in some time in the rural districts. Quite by chance the area I was allocated included my home village, so one morning I set off with a couple of nurses, <u>three male assistants and a suitcase full of medicines.</u> *suggests a lot of disease*

I was shocked by what I found. Either I had forgotten about the squalor of village life, or it had worsened during my absence. <u>The place was crawling with disease</u> and *personification - human qualities to objects* everybody was <u>living — surviving</u>, rather — in <u>acute</u> poverty. *differences* *extreme*
I found Veronica in the same hut she had grown up in. She was squatting over a smoking fire, fanning the flames with a piece of cardboard. There was a baby tied to
70 her back.

'Veronica,' I said. She turned round, startled. My immediate impression was that the ten years had told on her more than they should have.

'Okeke, is that you?' She peered at me through streaming eyes.

'How are you?' I asked.

'I'm still here, as you left me. <u>What should of happened</u> [sic] to me? Come, sit down, let me make you tea.' She indicated a stool. <u>I watched her as she busied</u> herself. When she finally sat down to feed the baby I asked her about herself. She shrugged.

'What am I to tell you? You heard that my parents died?'

80 'No, I didn't hear.'

'It's a long time now.'

'What about your brothers and sisters?'

'They are gone, all of them.'

'Where?'

'All over.' With her hand she made a semi-circle in the air.

'Do you hear from them at all?'

'What do they want with me? They have their own lives to lead.' She spoke without bitterness.

'Who is your husband?' I asked.

90   'You don't know him, he is not of our people.'

'How did you meet him?'

'He was in the North when the trouble broke out. They took everything he owned, he was lucky to escape alive. One day he showed up there. He had been walking for weeks and he was half-dead. I was alone here at the time. I looked after him, and when he got better he asked me to marry him. We have been together for one year now.

'Is he good to you?'

'He is a good man. He works hard in the fields, but he has no luck.'

'I'm sorry,' I said.

100   'No, don't be sorry for me. We are managing, and God has blessed us with a son. Is that not enough?'

'You would be better off in the city.'

'This is my home, Okeke. But what of you? You are a big man now, not so? Where is your wife?'

'I have no wife.'

'But why?'

'All the women I meet are only interested in money and cars.'

'I don't believe you.'

'It's true.'

lacking in information

110   I was in the village a month. I saw Veronica every day, and sometimes her husband. He was a good man, as she had said, if a bit simple. On the day I left I had to force her to accept a present of some money. It was as much as I could afford, but not as much as I would have liked to have been able to give her.

Is he just walking about money or would we have liked to have given her his world?

A few months after I got back to the city the war broke out. As she was in the fighting zone I lost contact with her again.

Three years passed before I could travel to the village again. This time I went alone. When I got there and saw all the destruction I could have wept. I had never imagined anything like it. I went straight to Veronica's hut. It was dark inside and bare save for a figure huddled on a mat on the ground.

he could never even think that life at home could be that bad.

120   'Veronica,' I called. She opened her eyes. I went over and knelt beside her. My eyes had become accustomed to the darkness. I saw at once that if I did not get her out of there quickly she would die.

'Okeke, welcome,' she said. I reached for her hand and held it. It was cold and limp.

'I'll get you out of here, don't worry,' I said.

'What for?'

'Veronica, if you stay here you'll die.'

She tried to sit up but I restrained her. 'Don't exert yourself, you need all your strength.'

130   'I was lying here thinking about you. I wanted to see you once more before I go.'

'I'm here now, and you're going to be alright.'

'Okeke, I won't live to see tomorrow. Nor do I want to. My husband is dead, and my child also. There is nothing left for me in this world.'

'You're still a young woman, in time you will forget this.'

'No, Okeke, listen to me. I don't want to live, you hear? Now that I have seen you I am happy. Go, and leave me in peace.'

She closed her eyes and turned her face to the wall. I gathered her up in my arms. She weighed no more than a ten-year-old child. She was dead before I reached my car.

140   I cried that night for the terrible waste. In the morning, just as the sun was rising, I carried her body down to the stream. And then I dug her a grave and buried her and afterwards I watched the flow of the stream until it was time for me to go away for the last time.

▼ Adewale Maja-Pearce

The author

Was born in London (1953). He grew up in Lagos, Nigeria. 'Veronica' is set in Nigeria, a country with troubled political history.

Financial development within the country has been limited to poverty.

The Necklace

She was one of those pretty, delightful girls who, apparently by some error of Fate, get themselves born the daughters of very minor civil servants. She had no dowry, no expectations, no means of meeting some rich, important man who would understand, love, and marry her. So she went along with a proposal made by a junior clerk in the Ministry of Education.

She dressed simply, being unable to afford anything better, but she was every whit as unhappy as any daughter of good family who has come down in the world. Women have neither rank nor class, and their beauty, grace, and charm do service for birthright and connections. Natural guile, instinctive elegance, and adaptability
10 are what determines their place in the hierarchy, and a girl of no birth to speak of may easily be the equal of any society lady.

She was unhappy all the time, for she felt that she was intended for a life of refinement and luxury. She was made unhappy by the run-down apartment they lived in, the peeling walls, the battered chairs, and the ugly curtains. Now all this, which any other woman of her station might never even have noticed, was torture to her and made her very angry. The spectacle of the young Breton peasant girl who did the household chores stirred sad regrets and impossible fancies. She dreamed of silent antechambers hung with oriental tapestries, lit by tall, bronze candelabras, and of two tall footmen in liveried breeches asleep in the huge armchairs, dozing in the
20 heavy heat of a stove. She dreamed of great drawing-rooms dressed with old silk, filled with fine furniture which showed off trinkets beyond price, and of pretty little parlours, filled with perfumes and just made for intimate talk at five in the afternoon with one's closest friends who would be the most famous and sought-after men of the day whose attentions were much coveted and desired by all women.

When she sat down to dinner at the round table spread with a three-day-old cloth, facing her husband who always lifted the lid of the soup-tureen and declared delightedly: 'Ah! Stew! Splendid! There's nothing I like better than a nice stew...', she dreamed of elegant dinners, gleaming silverware, and tapestries which peopled the walls with mythical characters and strange birds in enchanted forests; she
30 dreamed of exquisite dishes served on fabulous china plates, of pretty compliments whispered into willing ears and received with Sphinx-like smiles over the pink flesh of a trout or the wings of a hazel hen.

She had no fine dresses, no jewellery, nothing. And that was all she cared about; she felt that God had made her for such things. She would have given anything to be popular, envied, attractive, and in demand.

She had a friend who was rich, a friend from her convent days, on whom she never called now, for she was always so unhappy afterwards. Sometimes, for days on end, she would weep tears of sorrow, regret, despair, and anguish.

One evening her husband came home looking highly pleased with himself. In his hand
40 he brandished a large envelope.

'Look,' he said, 'I've got something for you.'

She tore the paper flap eagerly and extracted a printed card bearing these words:

'The Minister of Education and Madame Georges Ramponneau request the pleasure of the company of Monsieur and Madame Loisel at the Ministry Buildings on the evening of 18 January.'

Instead of being delighted as her husband had hoped, she tossed the invitation peevishly onto the table and muttered: 'What earthly use is that to me?'

'But, darling, I thought you'd be happy. You never go anywhere and it's an opportunity, a splendid opportunity! I had the dickens of a job getting hold of an invite. Everybody's after them; they're very much in demand and not many are handed out to us clerks. You'll be able to see all the big nobs there.'

50 She looked at him irritably and said shortly: 'And what am I supposed to wear if I do go?'

He had not thought of that. He blustered: 'What about the dress you wear for the theatre? It looks all right to me ...' The words died in his throat. He was totally disconcerted and dismayed by the sight of his wife who had begun to cry. Two large tears rolled slowly out of the corners of her eyes and down towards the sides of her mouth.

'What's up?' he stammered. 'What's the matter?'

Making a supreme effort, she controlled her sorrows and, wiping her damp cheeks, replied quite calmly: 'Nothing. It's just that I haven't got anything to wear and consequently I shan't be going to any reception. Give the invite to one of your
60 colleagues with a wife who is better off for clothes than I am.'

He was devastated. He went on: 'Oh come on, Mathilde. Look, what could it cost to get something suitable that would do for other occasions, something fairly simple?'

She thought for a few moments, working out her sums but also wondering how much she could decently ask for without drawing an immediate refusal and pained protests from her husband who was careful with his money. Finally, after some hesitation, she said: 'I can't say precisely, but I daresay I could get by on four hundred francs.'

He turned slightly pale, for he had been setting aside just that amount to buy a
70 gun and finance hunting trips the following summer in the flat landscape around Nanterre with a few friends who went shooting larks there on Sundays. But he said: 'Very well. I'll give you your four hundred francs. But do try and get a decent dress.'

The day of the reception drew near and Madame Loisel appeared sad, worried, anxious. Yet all her clothes were ready. One evening her husband said: 'What's up? You haven't half been acting funny these last few days.'

She replied: 'It vexes me that I haven't got a single piece of jewellery, not one stone, that I can put on. I'll look like a church mouse. I'd almost as soon not go to the reception.'

'Wear a posy,' he said. 'It's all the rage this year. You could get two or three
80 magnificent roses for ten francs.'

She was not convinced. 'No. ...There's nothing so humiliating as to look poor when you're with women who are rich.'

But her husband exclaimed: 'You aren't half silly! Look, go and see your friend, Madame Forestier, and ask her to lend you some jewellery. You know her well enough for that.'

She gave a delighted cry: 'You're right! I never thought of that!'

The next day she called on her friend and told her all about her problem. Madame Forestier went over to a mirror-fronted wardrobe, took out a large casket, brought it over, unlocked it, and said to Madame Loisel: 'Choose whatever you like.'

90   At first she saw bracelets, then a rope of pearls and a Venetian cross made of gold and diamonds admirably fashioned. She tried on the necklaces in the mirror, and could hardly bear to take them off and give them back. She kept asking: 'Have you got anything else?'

'Yes, of course. Just look. I can't say what sort of thing you'll like best.'

All of a sudden, in a black satinwood case, she found a magnificent diamond necklace, and her heart began to beat with immoderate desire. Her hands shook as she picked it up. She fastened it around her throat over her high-necked dress and sat looking at herself in rapture. Then, diffidently, apprehensively, she asked: 'Can you lend me this? Nothing else. Just this.'

100   'But of course.'

She threw her arms around her friend, kissed her extravagantly, and then ran home, taking her treasure with her.

The day of the reception arrived. Madame Loisel was a success. She was the prettiest woman there, elegant, graceful, radiant, and wonderfully happy. All the men looked at her, enquired who she was, and asked to be introduced. All the cabinet secretaries and under-secretaries wanted to waltz with her. She was even noticed by the Minister himself.

She danced ecstatically, wildly, intoxicated with pleasure, giving no thought to anything else, swept along on her victorious beauty and glorious success, and floating
110 on a cloud of happiness composed of the homage, admiration, and desire she evoked and the kind of complete and utter triumph which is so sweet to a woman's heart.

She left at about four in the morning. Since midnight her husband had been dozing in a small, empty side-room with three other men whose wives were having an enjoyable time.

He helped her on with her coat which he had fetched when it was time to go, a modest, everyday coat, a commonplace coat violently at odds with the elegance of her dress. It brought her down to earth, and she would have preferred to slip away quietly and avoid being noticed by the other women who were being arrayed in rich furs. But Loisel grabbed her by the arm: 'Wait a sec. You'll catch cold outside. I'll go
120 and get a cab.'

But she refused to listen and ran quickly down the stairs. When they were outside in the street, there was no cab in sight. They began looking for one, hailing all the cabbies they saw driving by in the distance.

They walked down to the Seine in desperation, shivering with cold. There, on the embankment, they at last found one of those aged nocturnal hackney cabs which only emerge in Paris after dusk, as if ashamed to parade their poverty in the full light of day. It bore them back to their front door in the rue des Martyrs, and they walked sadly up to their apartment. For her it was all over, while he was thinking that he would have to be at the Ministry at ten.

130   Standing in front of the mirror, she took off the coat she had been wearing over her shoulders, to get a last look at herself in all her glory. Suddenly she gave a cry. The necklace was no longer round her throat!

Her husband, who was already half undressed, asked: 'What's up?

She turned to him in a panic: 'I ... I ... Madame Forestier's necklace ... I haven't got it!'

He straightened up as if thunderstruck: 'What? ... But ... You can't have lost it!'

They looked in the pleats of her dress, in the folds of her coat, and in her pockets. They looked everywhere. They did not find it.

'Are you sure you still had it when you left the ballroom?' he asked.

140 'Yes, I remember fingering it in the entrance hall.'

'But if you'd lost it in the street, we'd have heard it fall. So it must be in the cab.'

'That's right. That's probably it. Did you get his number?'

'No. Did you happen to notice it?'

'No.'

They looked at each other in dismay. Finally Loisel got dressed again. 'I'm going to go back the way we came,' he said, 'to see if I can find it.' He went out. She remained as she was, still wearing her evening gown, not having the strength to go to bed, sitting disconsolately on a chair by the empty grate, her mind a blank.

150 Her husband returned at about seven o'clock. He had found nothing.

He went to the police station, called at newspaper offices where he advertised a reward, toured the cab companies, and tried anywhere where the faintest of hopes led him. She waited for him all day long in the same distracted condition, thinking of the appalling catastrophe which had befallen them.

Loisel came back that evening, hollow-cheeked and very pale. He had not come up with anything.

'Look,' he said, 'you'll have to write to your friend and say you broke the catch on her necklace and you are getting it repaired. That'll give us time to work out what we'll have to do.'

160 She wrote to his dictation.

A week later they had lost all hope.

Loisel, who had aged five years, said: 'We'll have to start thinking about replacing the necklace.'

The next day they took the case in which it had come and called on the jeweller whose name was inside. He looked through his order book.

'It wasn't me that sold the actual necklace. I only supplied the case.'

After this, they trailed round jeweller's shops, looking for a necklace just like the other one, trying to remember it, and both ill with worry and anxiety.

In a shop in the Palais Royal they found a diamond collar which they thought was 170 identical to the one they were looking for. It cost forty thousand francs. The jeweller was prepared to let them have it for thirty-six.

They asked him not to sell it for three days. And they got him to agree to take it back for thirty-four thousand if the one that had been lost turned up before the end of February.

Loisel had eighteen thousand francs which his father had left him. He would have to borrow the rest.

He borrowed the money, a thousand francs here, five hundred there, sometimes a hundred and as little as sixty. He signed notes, agreed to pay exorbitant rates of interest, resorted to usurers and the whole tribe of moneylenders. He mortgaged the rest of his life, signed papers without knowing if he would ever be able to honour his commitments, and then, sick with worry about the future, the grim poverty which stood ready to pounce, and the prospect of all the physical privation and mental torture ahead, he went round to the jeweller's to get the new necklace with the thirty-six thousand francs which he put on the counter.

When Madame Loisel took it round, Madame Forestier said in a huff: 'You ought really to have brought it back sooner. I might have needed it.'

She did not open the case, as her friend had feared she might. If she had noticed the substitution, what would she have thought? What would she have said? Would she not have concluded she was a thief?

Then began for Madame Loisel the grindingly horrible life of the very poor. But quickly and heroically, she resigned herself to what she could not alter: their appalling debt would have to be repaid. She was determined to pay. They dismissed the maid. They moved out of their apartment and rented an attic room.

She became used to heavy domestic work and all kinds of ghastly kitchen chores. She washed dishes, wearing down her pink nails on the greasy pots and saucepans. She washed the dirty sheets, shirts, and floorcloths by hand and hung them up to dry on a line; each morning she took the rubbish down to the street and carried the water up, pausing for breath on each landing. And, dressed like any working-class woman, she shopped at the fruiterer's, the grocer's, and the butcher's, with a basket over her arm, haggling, frequently abused and always counting every penny.

Each month they had to settle some accounts, renew others, and bargain for time.

Her husband worked in the evenings doing accounts for a shopkeeper and quite frequently sat up into the early hours doing copying work at five sous* a page.

They lived like this for ten years.

By the time ten years had gone by, they had repaid everything, with not a penny outstanding, in spite of the extortionate conditions and including the accumulated interest.

Madame Loisel looked old now. She had turned into the battling, hard, uncouth housewife who rules working-class homes. Her hair was untidy, her skirts were askew, and her hands were red. She spoke in a gruff voice and scrubbed floors on her hands and knees. But sometimes, when her husband had gone to the office, she would sit by the window and think of that evening long ago when she had been so beautiful and so admired.

What might not have happened had she not lost the necklace? Who could tell? Who could possibly tell? Life is so strange, so fickle! How little is needed to make or break us!

One Sunday, needing a break from her heavy working week, she went out for a stroll on the Champs-Elysées*. Suddenly she caught sight of a woman pushing a child in a pram. It was Madame Forestier, still young, still beautiful, and still attractive.

Madame Loisel felt apprehensive. Should she speak to her? Yes, why not? Now that she had paid in full, she would tell her everything. Why not? She went up to her.

'Hello, Jeanne.'

The friend did not recognize her and was taken aback at being addressed so familiarly by a common woman in the street. She stammered: 'But ... I'm sorry ... I don't know ... There's some mistake.'

'No mistake. I'm Madame Loisel.'

Her friend gave a cry: 'But my poor Mathilde, how you've changed!'

'Yes, I've been through some hard times since I saw you, very hard times. And it 230 was all on your account.'

'On my account? Whatever do you mean?'

'Do you remember that diamond necklace you lent me to go to the reception at the Ministry?'

'Yes. What about it?'

'Well I lost it.'

'Lost it? But you returned it to me.'

'No, I returned another one just like it. And we've been paying for it these past ten years. You know, it wasn't easy for us. We had nothing. ... But it's over and done with now, and I'm glad.'

240 Madame Forestier stopped. 'You mean you bought a diamond necklace to replace mine?'

'Yes. And you never noticed the difference, did you? They were exactly alike.' And she smiled a proud, innocent smile.

Madame Forestier looked very upset and, taking both her hands in hers, said:

'Oh, my poor Mathilde! But it was only an imitation necklace. It couldn't have been worth much more than five hundred francs! ...'

Guy de Maupassant

*Sous**: coin of very small value

*Champs Elysées**: famous street in Paris

A Hero

For Swami events took an unexpected turn. Father looked over the newspaper he was reading under the hall lamp and said, "Swami, listen to this: 'News is to hand of the bravery of a village lad who, while returning home by the jungle path, came face to face with a tiger …'" The paragraph described the fight the boy had with the tiger and his flight up a tree, where he stayed for half a day till some people came that way and killed the tiger.

After reading it through, Father looked at Swami fixedly and asked, "What do you say to that?"

Swami said, "I think he must have been a very strong and grown-up person, not at 10 all a boy. How could a boy fight a tiger?"

"You think you are wiser than the newspaper?" Father sneered. "A man may have the strength of an elephant and yet be a coward: whereas another may have the strength of a straw, but if he has courage he can do anything. Courage is everything, strength and age are not important."

Swami disputed the theory. "How can it be, Father? Suppose I have all the courage, what can I do if a tiger should attack me?"

"Leave alone strength, can you prove you have courage? Let me see if you can sleep alone tonight in my office room."

A frightful proposition, Swami thought. He had always slept beside his granny in 20 the passage, and any change in this arrangement kept him trembling and awake all night. He hoped at first that his father was only joking. He mumbled weakly, "Yes," and tried to change the subject; he said very loudly and with a great deal of enthusiasm, "We are going to admit even elders in our cricket club hereafter. We are buying brand-new bats and balls. Our captain has asked me to tell you …"

"We'll see about it later," Father cut in. "You must sleep alone hereafter." Swami realized that the matter had gone beyond his control: from a challenge it had become a plain command; he knew his father's tenacity at such moments.

"From the first of next month I'll sleep alone, Father."

"No, you must do it now. It is disgraceful sleeping beside granny or mother like a 30 baby. You are in the second form and I don't at all like the way you are being brought up," he said, and looked at his wife, who was rocking the cradle. "Why do you look at me while you say it?" she asked. "I hardly know anything about the boy."

"No, no, I don't mean you," father said.

"If you mean that your mother is spoiling him, tell her so; and don't look at me," she said, and turned away.

Swami's father sat gloomily gazing at the newspaper on his lap. Swami rose silently and tiptoed away to his bed in the passage. Granny was sitting up in her bed, and remarked, "Boy, are you already feeling sleepy? Don't you want a story?" Swami made wild gesticulations to silence his granny, but that good lady saw nothing. So 40 Swami threw himself on his bed and pulled the blanket over his face.

Granny said, "Don't cover your face. Are you really very sleepy?" Swami leant over and whispered, "Please, please, shut up, granny. Don't talk to me, and don't let anyone call me even if the house is on fire. If I don't sleep at once I shall perhaps die—" He turned over, curled, and snored under the blanket till he found his blanket pulled away.

Presently Father came and stood over him. "Swami, get up," he said. He looked like an apparition in the semi-darkness of the passage, which was lit by a cone of light from the hall. Swami stirred and groaned as if in sleep. Father said, "Get up, Swami." Granny pleaded, "Why do you disturb him?"

50   "Get up, Swami," he said for the fourth time, and Swami got up. Father rolled up his bed, took it under his arm, and said, "Come with me." Swami looked at his granny, hesitated for a moment, and followed his father into the office room. On the way he threw a look of appeal at his mother and she said, "Why do you take him to the office room? He can sleep in the hall, I think."

"I don't think so," Father said, and Swami slunk behind him with bowed head.

"Let me sleep in the hall, Father," Swami pleaded. "Your office room is very dusty and there may be scorpions behind your law books."

"There are no scorpions, little fellow. Sleep on the bench if you like."

"Can I have a lamp burning in the room?"

60   "No. You must learn not to be afraid of darkness. It is only a question of habit. You must cultivate good habits."

"Will you at least leave the door open?"

"All right. But promise you will not roll up your bed and go to your granny's side at night. If you do it, mind you, I will make you the laughing-stock of your school."

Swami felt cut off from humanity. He was pained and angry. He didn't like the strain of cruelty he saw in his father's nature. He hated the newspaper for printing the tiger's story. He wished that the tiger hadn't spared the boy, who didn't appear to be a boy after all, but a monster....

As the night advanced and the silence in the house deepened, his heart beat
70 faster. He remembered all the stories of devils and ghosts he had heard in his life. How often had his chum Mani seen the devil in the banyan tree at his street-end. And what about poor Munisami's father, who spat out blood because the devil near the river's edge slapped his cheek when he was returning home late one night. And so on and on his thoughts continued. He was faint with fear. A ray of light from the street lamp strayed in and cast shadows on the wall. Through the stillness all kinds of noises reached his ears — the ticking of the clock, rustle of trees, snoring sounds, and some vague night insects humming. He covered himself so completely that he could hardly breathe. Every moment he expected the devils to come up to carry him away; there was the instance of his old friend in the fourth class who suddenly disappeared and
80 was said to have been carried off by a ghost to Siam or Nepal ...

Swami hurriedly got up and spread his bed under the bench and crouched there. It seemed to be a much safer place, more compact and reassuring. He shut his eyes tight and encased himself in his blanket once again and unknown to himself fell asleep, and in sleep was racked with nightmares. A tiger was chasing him. His feet stuck to the ground. He desperately tried to escape but his feet would not move; the tiger was at his back, and he could hear its claws scratch the ground ... scratch, scratch, and then a light thud....Swami tried to open his eyes, but his eyelids would not open and the nightmare continued. It threatened to continue forever. Swami groaned in despair.

90   With a desperate effort he opened his eyes. He put his hand out to feel his granny's presence at his side, as was his habit, but he only touched the wooden leg of the bench. And his lonely state came back to him. He sweated with fright. And now what was this rustling? He moved to the edge of the bench and stared into the darkness. Something was moving down. He lay gazing at it in horror. His end had come. He realized that the devil would presently pull him out and tear him, and so why should he wait? As it came nearer he crawled out from under the bench, hugged it with all his might, and used his teeth on it like a mortal weapon ...

"Aiyo! Something has bitten me," went forth an agonized, thundering cry and was followed by a heavy tumbling and falling amidst furniture. In a moment Father, cook,
100   and a servant came in, carrying light.

And all three of them fell on the burglar who lay amidst the furniture with a bleeding ankle ....

Congratulations were showered on Swami next day. His classmates looked at him with respect, and his teacher patted his back. The headmaster said that he was a true scout. Swami had bitten into the flesh of one of the most notorious house-breakers of the district and the police were grateful to him for it.

The Inspector said, "Why don't you join the police when you are grown up?"

Swami said for the sake of politeness, "Certainly, yes," though he had quite made up his mind to be an engine driver, a railway guard, or a bus conductor later in life.

110   When he returned home from the club that night, Father asked, "Where is the boy?"

"He is asleep."

"Already!"

"He didn't have a wink of sleep the whole of last night," said his mother.

"Where is he sleeping?"

"In his usual place," Mother said casually. "He went to bed at seven-thirty."

"Sleeping beside his granny again!" Father said. "No wonder he wanted to be asleep before I could return home — clever boy!"

Mother lost her temper. "You let him sleep where he likes. You needn't risk his
120   life again. ..." Father mumbled as he went in to change: "All right, molly-coddle and spoil him as much as you like. Only don't blame me afterwards. ..."

Swami, following the whole conversation from under the blanket, felt tremendously relieved to hear that his father was giving him up.

R. K. Narayan

King Schahriar and his brother

(From The Arabian Nights)

'The Arabian Nights' (sometimes called 'The Thousand and One Nights') is the most famous collection of stories in the world. It was originally written in Arabic over a thousand years ago. 'King Schahriar and his brother' begins the cycle of stories and sets the scene for the rest.

In the chronicles of the ancient dynasty of the Sassanidae, who reigned for about four hundred years, from Persia to the borders of China, beyond the great river Ganges itself, we read the praises of one of the kings of this race, who was said to be the best monarch of his time. His subjects loved him, and his neighbors [sic] feared him, and when he died he left his kingdom in a more prosperous and powerful condition than any king had done before him.

The two sons who survived him loved each other tenderly, and it was a real grief to the elder, Schahriar, that the laws of the empire forbade him to share his dominions with his brother Schahzeman. Indeed, after ten years, during which this state of
10   things had not ceased to trouble him, Schahriar cut off the country of Great Tartary from the Persian Empire and made his brother king.

Now the Sultan Schahriar had a wife whom he loved more than all the world, and his greatest happiness was to surround her with splendour, and to give her the finest dresses and the most beautiful jewels. It was therefore with the deepest shame and sorrow that he accidentally discovered, after several years, that she had deceived him completely, and her whole conduct turned out to have been so bad, that he felt himself obliged to carry out the law of the land, and order the grand-vizir to put her to death. The blow was so heavy that his mind almost gave way, and he declared that he was quite sure that at bottom all women were as wicked as the sultana, if
20   you could only find them out, and that the fewer the world contained the better. So every evening he married a fresh wife and had her strangled the following morning before the grand-vizir, whose duty it was to provide these unhappy brides for the Sultan. The poor man fulfilled his task with reluctance, but there was no escape, and every day saw a girl married and a wife dead.

This behaviour caused the greatest horror in the town, where nothing was heard but cries and lamentations. In one house was a father weeping for the loss of his daughter, in another perhaps a mother trembling for the fate of her child; and instead of the blessings that had formerly been heaped on the Sultan's head, the air was now full of curses.

30   The grand-vizir himself was the father of two daughters, of whom the elder was called Scheherazade, and the younger Dinarzade. Dinarzade had no particular gifts to distinguish her from other girls, but her sister was clever and courageous in the highest degree. Her father had given her the best masters in philosophy, medicine, history and the fine arts, and besides all this, her beauty excelled that of any girl in the kingdom of Persia.

One day, when the grand-vizir was talking to his eldest daughter, who was his delight and pride, Scheherazade said to him, "Father, I have a favour to ask of you. Will you grant it to me?"

"I can refuse you nothing," replied he, "that is just and reasonable."

40 "Then listen," said Scheherazade. "I am determined to stop this barbarous practice of the Sultan's, and to deliver the girls and mothers from the awful fate that hangs over them."

"It would be an excellent thing to do," returned the grand-vizir, "but how do you propose to accomplish it?"

"My father," answered Scheherazade, "it is you who have to provide the Sultan daily with a fresh wife, and I implore you, by all the affection you bear me, to allow the honour to fall upon me."

"Have you lost your senses?" cried the grand-vizir, starting back in horror. "What has put such a thing into your head? You ought to know by this time what it means to be
50 the sultan's bride!"

"Yes, my father, I know it well," replied she, "and I am not afraid to think of it. If I fail, my death will be a glorious one, and if I succeed I shall have done a great service to my country."

"It is of no use," said the grand-vizir, "I shall never consent. If the Sultan was to order me to plunge a dagger in your heart, I should have to obey. What a task for a father! Ah, if you do not fear death, fear at any rate the anguish you would cause me."

"Once again, my father," said Scheherazade, "will you grant me what I ask?"

"What, are you still so obstinate?" exclaimed the grand-vizir. "Why are you so
60 resolved upon your own ruin?"

But the maiden absolutely refused to attend to her father's words, and at length, in despair, the grand-vizir was obliged to give way, and went sadly to the palace to tell the Sultan that the following evening he would bring him Scheherazade.

The Sultan received this news with the greatest astonishment.

"How have you made up your mind," he asked, "to sacrifice your own daughter to me?"

"Sire," answered the grand-vizir, "it is her own wish. Even the sad fate that awaits her could not hold her back."

"Let there be no mistake, vizir," said the Sultan. "Remember you will have to take
70 her life yourself. If you refuse, I swear that your head shall pay forfeit."

"Sire," returned the vizir. "Whatever the cost, I will obey you. Though a father, I am also your subject." So the Sultan told the grand-vizir he might bring his daughter as soon as he liked.

The vizir took back this news to Scheherazade, who received it as if it had been the most pleasant thing in the world. She thanked her father warmly for yielding to her wishes, and, seeing him still bowed down with grief, told him that she hoped he would never repent having allowed her to marry the Sultan. Then she went to prepare herself for the marriage, and begged that her sister Dinarzade should be sent for to speak to her.

80 When they were alone, Scheherazade addressed her thus:

"My dear sister; I want your help in a very important affair. My father is going to take me to the palace to celebrate my marriage with the Sultan. When his Highness receives me, I shall beg him, as a last favour, to let you sleep in our chamber, so that I may have your company during the last night I am alive. If, as I hope, he grants me my wish, be sure that you wake me an hour before the dawn, and speak to me in these words: 'My sister, if you are not asleep, I beg you, before the sun rises, to tell me one of your charming stories.' Then I shall begin, and I hope by this means to deliver the people from the terror that reigns over them." Dinarzade replied that she would do with pleasure what her sister wished.

90 When the usual hour arrived the grand-vizir conducted Scheherazade to the palace, and left her alone with the Sultan, who bade her raise her veil and was amazed at her beauty. But seeing her eyes full of tears, he asked what was the matter. "Sire," replied Scheherazade, "I have a sister who loves me as tenderly as I love her. Grant me the favour of allowing her to sleep this night in the same room, as it is the last we shall be together." Schahriar consented to Scheherazade's petition and Dinarzade was sent for.

An hour before daybreak Dinarzade awoke, and exclaimed, as she had promised, "My dear sister, if you are not asleep, tell me I pray you, before the sun rises, one of your charming stories. It is the last time that I shall have the pleasure of hearing you."

100 Scheherazade did not answer her sister, but turned to the Sultan. "Will your highness permit me to do as my sister asks?" said she.

"Willingly," he answered. So Scheherazade began.

cliffhanger

Section C

If —

If you can keep your head when all about you
    Are losing theirs and blaming it on you,
If you can trust yourself when all men doubt you,
    But make allowance for their doubting too;
5   If you can wait and not be tired by waiting,
    Or being lied about, don't deal in lies,
Or being hated, don't give way to hating,
    And yet don't look too good, nor talk too wise:

If you can dream — and not make dreams your master;
10   If you can think — and not make thoughts your aim;
If you can meet with Triumph and Disaster
    And treat those two impostors just the same;
If you can bear to hear the truth you've spoken
    Twisted by knaves to make a trap for fools,
15   Or watch the things you gave your life to, broken,
    And stoop and build 'em up with worn-out tools:

If you can make one heap of all your winnings
    And risk it on one turn of pitch-and-toss,
And lose, and start again at your beginnings
20   And never breathe a word about your loss;
If you can force your heart and nerve and sinew
    To serve your turn long after they are gone,
And so hold on when there is nothing in you
    Except the Will which says to them: 'Hold on!'

25   If you can talk with crowds and keep your virtue,
    Or walk with Kings — nor lose the common touch,
If neither foes nor loving friends can hurt you,
    If all men count with you, but none too much;
If you can fill the unforgiving minute
30   With sixty seconds' worth of distance run,
Yours is the Earth and everything that's in it,
    And — which is more — you'll be a Man, my son!

Rudyard Kipling

Prayer Before Birth

I am not yet born; O hear me.
Let not the bloodsucking bat or the rat or the stoat or the
    club-footed ghoul come near me.

I am not yet born, console me.
5   I fear that the human race may with tall walls wall me,
    with strong drugs dope me, with wise lies lure me,
        on black racks rack me, in blood-baths roll me.

I am not yet born; provide me
With water to dandle me, grass to grow for me, trees to talk
10   to me, sky to sing to me, birds and a white light
        in the back of my mind to guide me.

I am not yet born; forgive me
For the sins that in me the world shall commit, my words
    when they speak me, my thoughts when they think me,
15   my treason engendered by traitors beyond me,
            my life when they murder by means of my
            hands, my death when they live me.

I am not yet born; rehearse me
In the parts I must play and the cues I must take when
20   old men lecture me, bureaucrats hector me, mountains
        frown at me, lovers laugh at me, the white
            waves call me to folly and the desert calls
            me to doom and the beggar refuses
              my gift and my children curse me.

25   I am not yet born; O hear me,
Let not the man who is beast or who thinks he is God
    come near me.

I am not yet born; O fill me
With strength against those who would freeze my
30   humanity, would dragoon me into a lethal automaton,
        would make me a cog in a machine, a thing with
            one face, a thing, and against all those
              who would dissipate my entirety, would
                blow me like thistledown hither and
35   thither or hither and thither
                like water held in the
                  hands would spill me.

Let them not make me a stone and let them not spill me.
Otherwise kill me.

Louis MacNeice

 UG026701 - Anthology for Edexcel International GCSE and Certificate Qualifications in English Language
and Literature – Issue 2 – March 2012 © Pearson Education Limited 2012

Half-past Two

Once upon a schooltime
He did Something Very Wrong
(I forget what it was).

And She said he'd done
5   Something Very Wrong, and must
Stay in the school-room till half-past two.

(Being cross, she'd forgotten
She hadn't taught him Time.
He was too scared at being wicked to remind her.)

10   He knew a lot of time: he knew
Gettinguptime, timeyouwereofftime,
Timetogohomenowtime, TVtime,

Timeformykisstime (that was Grantime).
All the important times he knew,
15   But not half-past two.

He knew the clockface, the little eyes
And two long legs for walking,
But he couldn't click its language,

So he waited, beyond onceupona,
20   Out of reach of all the timefors,
And knew he'd escaped for ever

Into the smell of old chrysanthemums on Her desk,
Into the silent noise his hangnail made,
Into the air outside the window, into ever.

25   And then, *My goodness*, she said,
Scuttling in, *I forgot all about you.*
Run along or you'll be late.

So she slotted him back into schooltime,
And he got home in time for teatime,
30   Nexttime, notimeforthatnowtime,

But he never forgot how once by not knowing time,
He escaped into the clockless land for ever,
Where time hides tick-less waiting to be born.

U.A.Fanthorpe

Piano

Softly, in the dusk, a woman is singing to me;
Taking me back down the vista of years, till I see
A child sitting under the piano, in the boom of the tingling
    strings
5   And pressing the small, poised feet of a mother who smiles as she
      sings.

In spite of myself, the insidious mastery of song
Betrays me back, till the heart of me weeps to belong
To the old Sunday evenings at home, with winter outside
10 And hymns in the cozy parlor, the tinkling piano our guide.

So now it is vain for the singer to burst into clamor
With the great black piano appassionato. The glamour
Of childish days is upon me, my manhood is cast
Down in the flood of remembrance, I weep like a child for the
15   past.

D.H.Lawrence

 UG026701 - Anthology for Edexcel International GCSE and Certificate Qualifications in English Language and Literature - Issue 2 - March 2012 © Pearson Education Limited 2012

Hide and Seek

Call out. Call loud: 'I'm ready! Come and find me!'
The sacks in the toolshed smell like the seaside.
They'll never find you in this salty dark,
But be careful that your feet aren't sticking out.
5 Wiser not to risk another shout.
The floor is cold. They'll probably be searching
The bushes near the swing. Whatever happens
You mustn't sneeze when they come prowling in.
And here they are, whispering at the door;
10 You've never heard them sound so hushed before.
Don't breathe. Don't move. Stay dumb. Hide in your blindness.
They're moving closer, someone stumbles, mutters;
Their words and laughter scuffle, and they're gone.
But don't come out just yet; they'll try the lane
15 And then the greenhouse and back here again.
They must be thinking that you're very clever,
Getting more puzzled as they search all over.
It seems a long time since they went away.
Your legs are stiff, the cold bites through your coat;
20 The dark damp smell of sand moves in your throat.
It's time to let them know that you're the winner.
Push off the sacks. Uncurl and stretch. That's better!
Out of the shed and call to them: 'I've won!
Here I am! Come and own up I've caught you!'
25 The darkening garden watches. Nothing stirs.
The bushes hold their breath; the sun is gone.
Yes, here you are. But where are they who sought you?

Vernon Scannell

Sonnet 116 'Let me not to the marriage...'

Let me not to the marriage of true minds
Admit impediments; love is not love
Which alters when it alteration finds,
Or bends with the remover to remove.
5   O no, it is an ever-fixèd mark
That looks on tempests and is never shaken;
It is the star to every wandering bark,
Whose worth's unknown, although his height be taken.
Love's not Time's fool, though rosy lips and cheeks
10   Within his bending sickle's compass come;
Love alters not with his brief hours and weeks,
But bears it out even to the edge of doom.
    If this be error and upon me proved,
    I never writ, nor no man ever loved.

William Shakespeare

The Tyger

Tyger, Tyger, burning bright,
In the forests of the night:
What immortal hand or eye
Could frame thy fearful symmetry?

5   In what distant deeps or skies
Burnt the fire of thine eyes?
On what wings dare he aspire?
What the hand dare seize the fire?

And what shoulder, & what art,
10 Could twist the sinews of thy heart?
And when thy heart began to beat,
What dread hand? & what dread feet?

What the hammer? what the chain,
In what furnace was thy brain?
15 What the anvil? what dread grasp
Dare its deadly terrors clasp!

When the stars threw down their spears
And waterd heaven with their tears:
Did he smile his work to see?
20 Did he who made the Lamb make thee?*

Tyger, Tyger burning bright,
In the forests of the night:
What immortal hand or eye
Dare frame thy fearful symmetry?

William Blake

*Did he who made the Lamb make thee**: God

My Last Duchess
Ferrara

That's my last Duchess painted on the wall,
Looking as if she were alive. I call
That piece a wonder, now: Frà Pandolf's hands
Worked busily a day, and there she stands.
5   Will't please you sit and look at her? I said
'Frà Pandolf' by design, for never read
Strangers like you that pictured countenance,
The depth and passion of its earnest glance,
But to myself they turned (since none puts by
10   The curtain I have drawn for you, but I)
And seemed as they would ask me, if they durst,
How such a glance came there; so, not the first
Are you to turn and ask thus. Sir, 'twas not
Her husband's presence only, called that spot
15   Of joy into the Duchess' cheek: perhaps
Frà Pandolf chanced to say 'Her mantle laps
Over my lady's wrist too much,' or 'Paint
Must never hope to reproduce the faint
Half-flush that dies along her throat': such stuff
20   Was courtesy, she thought, and cause enough
For calling up that spot of joy. She had
A heart — how shall I say? — too soon made glad,
Too easily impressed; she liked whate'er
She looked on, and her looks went everywhere.
25   Sir, 'twas all one! My favour at her breast,
The dropping of the daylight in the West,
The bough of cherries some officious fool
Broke in the orchard for her, the white mule
She rode with round the terrace — all and each
30   Would draw from her alike the approving speech,
Or blush, at least. She thanked men, — good! but thanked
Somehow — I know not how — as if she ranked
My gift of a nine-hundred-years-old name
With anybody's gift. Who'd stoop to blame
35   This sort of trifling? Even had you skill
In speech — (which I have not) — to make your will
Quite clear to such an one, and say, 'Just this
Or that in you disgusts me; here you miss,
Or there exceed the mark' — and if she let
40   Herself be lessoned so, nor plainly set
Her wits to yours, forsooth, and made excuse,
— E'en then would be some stooping; and I choose
Never to stoop. Oh sir, she smiled, no doubt,
Whene'er I passed her; but who passed without
45   Much the same smile? This grew; I gave commands;
Then all smiles stopped together. There she stands
As if alive. Will't please you rise? We'll meet
The company below, then. I repeat,
The Count your master's known munificence

50   Is ample warrant that no just pretence
      Of mine for dowry will be disallowed;
      Though his fair daughter's self, as I avowed
      At starting, is my object. Nay, we'll go
      Together down, sir. Notice Neptune, though,
55   Taming a sea-horse, thought a rarity,
      Which Claus of Innsbruck cast in bronze for me!

                                        Robert Browning

A Mother in a Refugee Camp

No Madonna and Child could touch
Her tenderness for a son
She soon would have to forget. . . .
The air was heavy with odors of diarrhea,
5   Of unwashed children with washed-out ribs
And dried-up bottoms waddling in labored steps
Behind blown-empty bellies. Other mothers there
Had long ceased to care, but not this one:
She held a ghost-smile between her teeth,
10   and in her eyes the memory
Of a mother's pride. . . . She had bathed him
And rubbed him down with bare palms.
She took from their bundle of possessions
A broken comb and combed
15   The rust-colored hair left on his skull
And then—humming in her eyes—began carefully to part it.
In their former life this was perhaps
A little daily act of no consequence
Before his breakfast and school; now she did it
20   Like putting flowers on a tiny grave.

Chinua Achebe

Please note the American spelling of 'odors' 'diarrhea' 'labored' and 'colored'.
(English spellings: odours, diarrhoea, laboured and coloured.)

Do not go gentle into that good night

Do not go gentle into that good night,
Old age should burn and rave at close of day;
Rage, rage against the dying of the light.

Though wise men at their end know dark is right,
5   Because their words had forked no lightning they
Do not go gentle into that good night.

Good men, the last wave by, crying how bright
Their frail deeds might have danced in a green bay,
Rage, rage against the dying of the light.

10   Wild men who caught and sang the sun in flight,
And learn, too late, they grieved it on its way,
Do not go gentle into that good night.

Grave men, near death, who see with blinding sight
Blind eyes could blaze like meteors and be gay,
15   Rage, rage against the dying of the light.

And you, my father, there on the sad height,
Curse, bless, me now with your fierce tears, I pray.
Do not go gentle into that good night.
Rage, rage against the dying of the light.

Dylan Thomas

Remember

Remember me when I am gone away,
    Gone far away into the silent land;
    When you can no more hold me by the hand,
Nor I half turn to go yet turning stay.
5   Remember me when no more day by day
    You tell me of our future that you planned:
    Only remember me; you understand
It will be late to counsel then or pray.
Yet if you should forget me for a while
10   And afterwards remember, do not grieve:
    For if the darkness and corruption leave
    A vestige of the thoughts that once I had,
Better by far you should forget and smile
    Than that you should remember and be sad.

Christina Rossetti

UG026701 – Anthology for Edexcel International GCSE and Certificate Qualifications in English Language and Literature – Issue 2 – March 2012 © Pearson Education Limited 2012

Acknowledgments

Edexcel wishes to thank the following for their kind permission to reproduce copyright material.

Section A

Touching the Void by Joe Simpson, published by Jonathan Cape. Reprinted by permission of The Random House Group Ltd

On The Beach © RNLI

Climate Change: The Facts by Kate Ravilious, © Guardian News and Media Limited

Reproduced with permission, *A GAME OF POLO WITH A HEADLESS GOAT* published by Andre Deutsch © Emma Levine 2000

A Passage to Africa by George Alagiah © Little, Brown Book Group

The Explorer's Daughter by Kari Herbert, reproduced by permission Penguin Classic— Aitken Alexander Associates Ltd

Explorers, or Boys Messing About? by Steve Morris, 28 January 2003 © Guardian News and Media Limited

Taking On the World by Ellen MacArthur (Michael Joseph, 2002) © Ellen MacArthur, 2002, reproduced by permission of A P Watt Ltd. on behalf of Offshore Challenges Ltd.

Chinese Cinderella by Adeline Yen Mah, Penguin © Adeline Yen Mah, 1999

Section B

Disabled — The Poems of Wilfred Owen, Wordsworth Edition

Out Out from The Poetry Of Robert Frost edited by Edward Connery Lathem, © 1916, 1969 by Henry Holt and Company, © 1944 by Robert Frost. Reprinted by permission of Henry Holt and Company, LLC — For Britain and Commonwealth Rights reprinted by permission of The Random House Group Ltd.

Refugee Blues from Collected Poems by W H Auden, 2004, © Faber and Faber Ltd.

An Unknown Girl by Moniza Alvi from Split World: Poems 1990-2005 (Bloodaxe Books, 2007)

Electricity Comes to Cocoa Bottom by Marcia Douglas, 1998, Peepal Tree Press Ltd

Charlotte Gray by Sebastian Faulks, 1999. Reprinted by permission of the Random House Group Limited

Veronica from Loyalties and Other Stories © Adewale Maja-Pearce, 1986, Longman Publisher

The Necklace from *A Day in the Country and Other Stories*, Guy De Maupassant, translated by David Coward, OUP

A Hero from Under the Banyan Tree by R K Narayan, published by William Heinemann. Reprinted by permission of The Randon House Group Ltd.

King Schahriar and his brother from *The Arabian Nights*, reproduced under the terms of the 'Project Gutenberg License'

Section C

If — 2001, © Rudyard Kipling, Penguin Classic

Prayer Before Birth from Selected Poems — 2007, Louis MacNeice, Faber and Faber

Half-past Two © U A Fanthorpe. First published in Neck-Verse (Peterloo Poets, 1992)

Piano from The Top 500 Poems — 1992, D H Lawrence, Editor William Harman, Columbia University

Hide and Seek from The Collected Poems 1950-93, Vernon Scannell, Robson Books Limited

Sonnet 116 — Shakespeare's Sonnets — 1999, © Shakespeare, Penguin Classic

La Belle Dame Sans Merci — 2007, © John Keats, Penguin Classic

Poem at Thirty-Nine by Alice Walker from *Horses Make a Landscape Look More Beautiful*, reproduced by permission of David Higham Associates Limited

Telephone Conversation © Wole Soyinka, from A Selection of African Poetry, K E Senanu and T Vincent, Longman Publisher

Once Upon a Time from The Fisherman's Invocation, Gabriel Okara © Ethiope Publishing Corporation

War Photographer by Carol Ann Duffy from *Standing Female Nude*, published by Anvil Press Poetry in 1985

The Tyger — 2006, © William Blake, Penguin Classic

My Last Duchess -2000, © Robert Browning, Penguin Classic

A Mother in a Refugee Camp by Chinua Achebe, 2005, Carcanet Press Limited

Do Not Go Gentle into That Good Night from *Selected Poems*: Dylan Thomas, Penguin Classic

Remember from Selected Poems: Rossetti. By permission of Louisiana State University Press

Every effort has been made to contact copyright holders to obtain their permission for the use of copyright material. Edexcel will, if notified, be happy to rectify any errors or omissions and include any such rectifications in future editions.

db190312G:\WORDPROC\LT\PD\INTERNATIONAL GCSE TSM\UG026701 INTERNATIONAL GCSE ANTHOLOGY - ENGLISH LANG (SPEC A) & ENGLISH LIT ISSUE 2\UG026701 INTERNATIONAL GCSE ANTHOLOGY - ENGLISH LANG (SPEC A) & ENGLISH LIT ISSUE 2.DOC.1-78/0

76   UG026701 - Anthology for Edexcel International GCSE and Certificate Qualifications in English Language and Literature – Issue 2 – March 2012 © Pearson Education Limited 2012